D1372511

Steady, Old Man!

Steady, Old Man!

*Don't You Know
There's a War On?*

DEREK BOND

LEO COOPER
London

First published 1990 by Leo Cooper

Leo Cooper is an independent imprint of the
Octopus Publishing Group, Michelin House,
81 Fulham Road, London SW3 6RB

LONDON   MELBOURNE   AUCKLAND

Copyright © Derek Bond 1990

ISBN 0 85052 046 0

A CIP catalogue record for this book
is available from the British Library

Photoset in Linotron Sabon by
Rowland Phototypesetting Ltd,
Bury St Edmunds, Suffolk

Printed in Great Britain by
Butler and Tanner Ltd, Frome, Somerset

Contents

To my darling Annie

Illustrations

Prologue

Convinced that I was going to be an ace newspaper man, I left Haberdashers' Aske's Hampstead School at sixteen as soon as I had achieved a modest School Certificate at the second attempt and became a part-time reporter on the *Golders Green Gazette*, whilst studying shorthand and typing at Pitmans.

My father had pleaded with me to continue my education at least until I was eighteen but, of course, I knew better. Today my father would have been called a Senior Sales Executive but in those days he was more honestly called a Commercial Traveller. He sold cloth but he sold a great deal of it so we were comparatively comfortable. Mother was a marvellous hostess and a superb cook. Our house in Hampstead Garden Suburb was always full of guests. One regular at Sunday luncheon was a widower called Tom Dunning, the Registrar of Friendly Societies – the equivalent of today's Certification Officer who is responsible to the Government for the proper conduct of Trades Union affairs. He had a razor sharp mind and a wicked wit. There was nothing he enjoyed more than drawing me into a complex political argument and then challenging my reasoning on all the points I thought I had made with irrefutable logic during our debate. Had he lived, I think he would have been wryly amused when I became President of Equity.

When my father discovered that I was showing more interest in my nubile classmates at Pitmans than in typing rubbish about 'The Big Brown Fox' he gave me a thoroughly deserved dressing down and accused me of wasting my life!

In a pique of hurt pride I swept off and applied for a job with Brown Shipley & Company, Merchant Bankers, which was advertised in the *Daily Telegraph*. I sat a very stiff examination and, to my astonishment, got the job. I was appointed Junior Postal Clerk at thirty shillings a week.

I abandoned the ace reporter role and adjusted my dream. I was to be a City tycoon! On the 'never-never' system I bought a businessman's suit from Hector Powe, an Anthony Eden hat, some kid-leather gloves and a very expensive umbrella. I even bought a fresh carnation each day from a flower seller outside the Corn Exchange until I was told by my superiors that it was 'unsuitable'! My 'Walter Mitty' image having been shattered, I lost all interest in the job.

My mother was an excellent amateur actress and deservedly the 'star' of the Finchley Amateur Dramatic Society. The Society had a reasonably high standard. They called themselves 'The Fads' and the leading lights enjoyed nicknames like Mig, Blob, Babs and Doffy. After attending a very demanding and competitive audition, I was cast as 'Maudleyn' in their production of *Richard of Bordeaux*. This was surprising because the master in charge of Drama at Haberdashers had been besotted with Gilbert and Sullivan and those of us interested in straight theatre were reduced to play-readings and I had never before set foot on any stage.

My modest success as Maudleyn went straight to my head and now I *knew* that all along I was destined to be an actor. I recruited mother as an ally, ignored my eldest brother's opinion that I was turning into a 'fairy' and confronted my father with my 'dramatic' decision. With admirable self-restraint he agreed to give me one year from the day I got my first job.

'But if you come to me for one penny during that year, my boy, I'll see to it that you get a proper job!'

For weeks I trekked up to the West End, attending audition

after audition without success and searching for an agent. One hard-bitten old agent in Cambridge Circus called Miriam Warner nearly reduced me to tears by saying: 'You look a nice young boy. Why don't you go home to mother?'

I looked so shattered that she took pity on me and got me a job in one of the first TV plays ever performed. This was in February, 1938, at Alexandra Palace. I played a robot in *R.U.R.* by Karel Capek. I was paid five guineas for three days' rehearsal and two live performances. Attached to my contract was a slip in red print which read as follows:

> All artists appearing in Television Programmes
> are particularly asked to cooperate with the
> Corporation in avoiding any reference to:
> Physical deformities or diseases.
> Religious subjects or quotations.
> Drunkenness or immorality of any kind.

I felt comparatively safe in signing the contract, as all I had to say in the play was the word 'Yes'!

The BBC could only afford two robots, whereas the play demanded hordes of them, so we endeavoured to appear to be at least *one* horde by sprinting round behind the camera over and over again to confront the mad scientist who was ordering us to 'Kill the Humans!' 'Yes!' we declared in flat robot-like tones and then rushed round behind the camera for a repeat performance. I was supposed to utter at least six 'Yeses' but only managed two because I tripped over my clumsy linoleum boots after my second performance and lay prone and helpless behind the camera for the rest of the transmission.

With experience, I had become an accomplished liar at auditions. For example, I had promoted the Finchley Amateur Dramatic Society to the Finchley Repertory Company. There were so many repertory companies at that time that I got away with it and bluffed myself into a job as understudy and ASM in a pre-London tour of *As Husbands Go*, starring Hugh Wakefield, who was also the Actor Manager, Jeanne de Casalis, Vera Lennox and Morris Harvey. I was paid the very handsome sum of £5 a week to understudy Bruce Seton and James Carney and be ASM.

At first I was very nervous of being found out as an amateur, but by sheer bluff I got away with it and learnt my job rapidly as I went along. There was a lesbian Stage Manager who was most helpful, but she was not popular with the stars and was sacked at the end of the tour. I took over. I became Stage Manager in London in my first professional job. I think it was mainly because I knew the show and I had got on very well with all the cast – especially Jeanne de Casalis who I had helped with her study when she was having difficulties with her script.

Before coming into the Garrick Theatre in London, it was decided to have two furniture removers on stage at the beginning of the second act for plot reasons. I was to be one of them *and* I was given a line! At the opening of the Act I was discovered on stage leaning on some new furniture with a fag drooping from my mouth. I was wearing corduroy trousers tied below the knee with string, a green baize apron, full theatrical make-up and I even went to the length of sticking my cigarette to my lower lip with spirit gum so I could let my mouth droop open. The other furniture remover entered and said: 'Come on, Dopey!'

My witty reply was, 'All right, Snow White!'

It never got a titter in spite of my trying every inflection possible with four words. Never mind! I was eighteen! I was playing in the West End! The world was my oyster!

One matinee day I was rushing out of the Stage Door of the Garrick Theatre to get a pint of beer and a sandwich after laying out the props when my father's car drew up outside. He was with a business colleague and they had both clearly had a very good morning at the pub. I ducked out of sight as father led his friend up to the hoarding by the theatre entrance and pointed out my name in tiny letters at the bottom of the playbill. His friend slapped father on the back and as they moved off I felt quite emotional as father gave a proud backwards glance at the hoarding. I never confessed that I'd seen him.

At the end of the three-month London run I was given an audition at Spotlight for the job of Stage Manager and Juvenile Lead with the Colchester Repertory Company. Colchester Repertory had one of the highest reputations in the country, although it was small and totally without subsidy at that time. The audition was for their summer season at the Prince's Theatre, Clacton. In my new-found confidence (or possibly arrogance?) it was no surprise to me that I got the job – after all, I now had West End experience!

Later, Robert Digby, who had founded the Company a year earlier, told me that he had only employed me because I tripped over the carpet entering the room and showered his desk with my Anthony Eden hat, my gloves, umbrella and my copy of *The Stage* – carefully camouflaged in *The Times*. For some perverse reason he found my gaucheness enchanting.

The summer season consisted of comedies such as *Third Time Lucky* by Arnold Ridley, *Full House* by Ivor Novello and *Hay Fever* by Noël Coward. Regretfully even these offerings appeared to be rather over the heads of the Clacton holiday-makers of 1938 and we were all thankful when the season ended and we returned to Colchester. All except me that is. I was acutely aware of my own inexperience and the much more critical audience we'd be facing at the Albert Hall in Colchester.

My fears were confirmed during my first week. I was playing the juvenile lead in *Hay Fever* and, although I had played it at Clacton, I was extremely nervous performing before regular repertory supporters. The men's dressing room was a long narrow corridor of a room partitioned off by plyboard from the audience's gentlemen's lavatory. We were asked to remember that our audience might well overhear us during the interval but no such warning could, of course, be given to the paying customers. During the first interval on the Monday night I was repairing my over-elaborate make-up when I heard the ringing tones of a member of our audience, clearly from the Officers' Mess at the Garrison, backed by a noisy cascade of pee, interrupted by rip-roaring farts, 'Don't like the new young fella! Face like a girl's and can't hear a bloody word he says!'

Those were, without exception, the most effective 'notes' I have ever been given in my professional career!

Stage managing weekly Rep and playing juvenile leads as well was almost an impossibility. I had one assistant, Bay White, straight from RADA but worth her weight in gold, one stage carpenter aided by a rather simple son, one electrician who enjoyed all the pubs in the High Street and the excellent Anthony Waller, the talented set designer who later was to become Head of Design at ATV.

In weekly Rep the actors worked a good seven-hour day six days a week, plus all their hours of study. The Stage Management team worked a twelve-hour day six days a week and didn't even have Sunday off. Having been up all hours striking the old set after the two Saturday shows we went to the theatre first thing on Sunday morning to help Anthony Waller wheel the new set on a handbarrow from the Scene Dock, which was in an old Scout hut a good mile away, to the theatre. We had to make several journeys dodging through the traffic and praying that it wouldn't rain. The new set was usually roughly set up by 11.30 when Robert Digby would arrive to pick me up in his car. We then set off to paste up posters in all the surrounding small towns and villages. Bob Digby thought it necessary to drop off handbills in nearly every pub and thought it impolite to ask the landlord to display a bill without buying at least a pint of beer. By the time we had worked our way back to Colchester near closing time the posters went up at some very erratic angles.

The strain of maintaining that régime on top of learning my lines for leading juvenile parts proved too much for me. The final straw was on the Monday night of *The Breadwinner* by Somerset Maugham. The electrician had repaired to the pub without warning, leaving me to wire up an entirely new lighting batten demanded by the producer in his final notes.

My limited knowledge of electrical wiring meant that it took me right up beyond the half-hour call to complete, albeit hazardously, and I was shaking with fatigue as I hurried to make up. During the performance I made an entrance to centre stage and 'dried' stone cold. In my despair I did the unforgiveable and exited hurriedly – muttering 'I've a lot of things to do!' – leaving my fellow actors on stage in a state of chaos.

Bob Digby sent for me the following morning. I was filled with shame over my behaviour and thought I would get my bit in first.

'Before you say anything, Bob, I want to give in my notice!'

'Don't be such a bloody young fool! I've already engaged a stage manager who is coming next week. You are to remain as juvenile lead at an increased salary of £4 a week! Now for God's sake come and have a drink!'

From then on I enjoyed every moment at Colchester apart from the 1938 pantomime. I was cast as Prince Charming in *Cinderella* and was required to sing 'Stay in my arms, Cinderella'. My only experience of singing had been giving my impression of Bing Crosby groaning 'Buddy – Can You Spare a Dime' at family parties. It was decided that I should be sent to a local vicar who gave singing lessons. It became clear to me very early on that the vicar was more interested in my body than my vocal chords and I spent most of the lessons running round the piano trying to protect my honour. At the first dress rehearsal I stepped forward wearing my powdered periwig, satin breeches and silver-buckled shoes and gave tongue. Before I had finished the first chorus the entire company was helpless with laughter. Trevor Howard, the Demon King, totally destroyed his make-up with tears streaming down his cheeks. It was decided to cut the song.

Anthony Waller was in despair because I was singing in front of a roller-cloth of a palace corridor while he and his students were setting up the ballroom set behind it. The producer, Hal Stewart, turned to me.

'Now, Derek, I know you can do this! I'll have the music

played louder and you'll just have to walk up and down thinking romantically of Cinderella!'

I was still at that stage of inexperience that when I lacked confidence I just didn't know what to do with my hands. Hal Stewart gave me a snuff box to play with. As I walked up and down in front of the roller-cloth on the first night, alternately sighing romantically and taking pinches of snuff, I got the biggest laugh of the evening. I continued to do so for the next two performances until I started to play for the laughs! This reduced the audience to embarrassed silence.

Bob Digby had his faults, such as a liking for alcohol and a very short fuse when he had had plenty, but he also had that very rare quality of inspiring those around him with his own enthusiasm. He was fanatical about the Rep and if he hadn't been it could never have survived. He didn't only inspire the Rep company itself but the whole business community of Colchester to support us, even the City Council which he miraculously persuaded to come up with a grant when such things were little known. When he managed to persuade the BBC to broadcast our production of *Outward Bound* he exploited it to the full for months afterwards. We got very good notices and from then on we were billed as THE COLCHESTER REPERTORY COMPANY OF BROADCASTING FAME!

We were all so involved with the Rep and its success that we became almost unaware of the unpleasant things that were happening in the big outside world. As a nation, I think we all had wanted to believe Chamberlain when he returned from Munich with his pathetic piece of paper signed by Adolf Hitler and mouthing platitudes like 'Peace in Our Time!'

It came as a great shock to us in August, 1939, when we were once again doing our Summer Season at Clacton that we learnt that Molotov and Ribbentrop had signed a Non-Aggression Pact between Communist Russia and Nazi Germany. I never knew whether Bob was a Party member but he was certainly a Communist. I remember so very vividly the day when he brought us the news. Trevor Howard and I were running a Tombola stall at a Garden Party run by all the

Clacton Summer Shows for local charities. Bob came up to us grey-faced.

'I can't bloody believe it! Hitler and Stalin have signed a Pact! This means a bloody war!'

He was right of course.

On Sunday, 27 August some very rich Repertory supporters who lived in a magnificent country mansion near Coggeshall and whose names I have shamefully forgotten gave a 'Waterloo' Ball. They engaged three bands, imported crates of champagne and invited all their friends including the whole Repertory Company. The men wore full evening dress and the girls their best ball gowns. It was a riotously successful party. At least I think it was. I rather lost touch with events before the transport was assembled to take us all back to Clacton. Furthermore I had disappeared. A thorough and rather desperate search was organized and Bob was just about to call the police to drag the ornamental lake when I was discovered fast asleep on the billiard table with the cover drawn over me like a bedsheet.

On Friday, 1 September the Germans invaded Poland from the west and the Russians from the east. In England the Blackout was imposed. I wasn't playing that particular week and I can remember Bob and myself standing outside the theatre in Station Road waving dimmed-out torches at the panic-stricken holiday-makers fleeing to the railway station shouting, 'We're open – we're open!' There were six in the audience that night.

On Saturday, 2 September, as our train, packed with civilians and troops, drew into Liverpool Street Station, we saw the barrage balloons floating like vast sinister sausages around the City. I think we all felt a mixture of fear and excitement. Fear because we thought Bertrand Russell might have been right when he had forecast that London would be wiped out on the first day of a war. Excitement because we were young.

My eldest brother, Kenneth, who was a Regular Officer in the RAF, had been posted to India, but on that Sunday morning the rest of the family, mother, father, middle brother

Greville, Tom Dunning and I gathered at eleven o'clock round our large wireless set, which looked like the West End of York Minster, to listen to the Prime Minister in his weary funereal tones declaring war on Germany. As he finished speaking we heard the wail of the first Air Raid siren of World War Two and we all climbed rather sheepishly under our solid mahogany dining table. Nothing at all happened and shortly afterwards the All Clear sounded and we emerged even more sheepishly. My father sighed.

'Oh well! I suppose we'd all better have a drink!'

I

The King's Shilling

After the drama of that first Air Raid Warning the days that followed were decidedly anti-climactic for the majority of the population. The Territorials, Reservists, Police Reserve, ARP (Air Raid Precautions) personnel and other volunteer units including the FANYs were called up. The FANYs – the First Aid Nursing Yeomanry – received a very cryptic telegram – COMPLETE FANY!

Out of the woodwork of our society emerged a number of people who couldn't wait to get into uniform and boss the rest of the nation around. Some years later in the real emergency many of them showed tremendous courage as Air Raid Wardens, firemen and nurses, but at first the uniforms rather went to the heads of lower middle-class people who had hitherto been disadvantaged by a rigidly class-ridden society. For a short time the blessed English sense of humour and anarchical rejection of authority faltered.

Without a doubt Air Raid Wardens were the worst and made themselves extremely unpopular enforcing the Blackout. One, at least, got his come-uppance. It was in Old Compton Street, Soho. A warden spotted some light shining from a first floor window. He rang the bell – keeping his finger firmly on it until the door opened to reveal a somewhat breathless busty blonde wearing nothing but a diaphanous negligee and a feather boa.

'Yes, dearie? What can I do for you?'

With some difficulty the Warden shifted his gaze from her ample bosoms.

'Madam – there's a little chink at your window!'

'Little Chink be buggered! That's the Japanese Ambassador!'

Paradoxically, one of the most difficult things to do in September, 1939, was to join the Forces. None of the Services wanted recruits at first because the nation was so woefully unprepared for war. After several unsuccessful attempts at Recruiting Centres, I settled for being a stretcher bearer in Hampstead. After rapid courses in First Aid, we spent night after night on standby, sleeping in unheated school gymnasiums in the bitter cold waiting for Hitler to strike. This was the 'phoney' war and it was extremely boring. It wasn't to last.

In October there was a BBC announcement of typical pomposity saying that there were 'vacancies for men of the right height standard and aged 20 or over in the Brigade of Guards'. I wasn't 20 until January but I decided to lie about my age and 'apply for a vacancy'.

Ever since I had slept all night in the Mall in 1935 to have a front place for the Procession on the occasion of King George V's Silver Jubilee I had developed an obsession about the Brigade of Guards. I didn't just admire their precision at drill but I had read book after book about the First World War and the Guards' valiant part in it. I wanted to be a Guardsman very much.

The Recruiting Centre at Wellington Barracks was thronged with tall men from all walks of life. The process of 'applying for a vacancy' was to fill up a form, bend over in front of the Medical Officer so that he could peer up your bum for piles, take the Oath, receive the King's Shilling and be told to report with a toothbrush to the Guards' Depot at Caterham on the following day without fail. Failure to appear would be Desertion Whilst On Active Service!

It wasn't until I got home and told my parents what I had done that I began to have doubts. Mother burst into tears and father was furious – not so much for what I had done but because I hadn't consulted him first. He couldn't understand why I hadn't just waited to be called up like everyone else. I pointed out that he had volunteered in the First World War and became a Sergeant in the Sappers in charge of steam lorries. I wanted to be an infantry soldier. This floored him at first but he then went on to paint a picture of the tough life I had taken on in the Guards. I didn't believe him. I should have done.

As I went through the barrack gates at Caterham my heart was in my mouth. I was almost sick with nerves. My first impression was of intolerable noise. Everyone seemed to be shouting at the tops of their voices and stamping their feet as if they wanted to fracture the tarmac of the barrack square. There were about a dozen squads of recruits being chased round the square by NCOs who seemed to be in the final stages of apoplexy. It was very alarming and it didn't help when the sergeant in charge of our party of new recruits said: 'We'll have you lot of idle bleeders on there tomorrow! Lucky, ain't yer?'

We were to learn that the word 'idle' was constantly on the lips of Guards NCOs, together with the word 'shower'. We were, of course, 'a very idle shower!' and ''orrible little men!'

The sergeant attempted to march us to the Quartermaster's Stores. As we stumbled over our own and other people's feet and got our arms hopelessly out of 'synch' with our legs the sergeant was almost reduced to tears. At the stores we were issued with Service Dress and puttees, two pairs of boots, denim fatigues, gym shoes, shorts and vest, army shirts, under-clothes, Service Dress caps and fore-and-aft caps known to Guardsmen as 'cunt' caps.

We were then marched, if you could call it that, to our barrack room. Ours was on the first floor of a red-brick Victorian building. There were iron beds with straw palliasses on either side of the long narrow room. The main feature of the room was a highly polished floor which I, for one, was to learn to hate.

We were then introduced to our Trained Soldier. Each

barrack room had a Trained Soldier who had to be addressed as such. It wasn't really a rank but he had full authority over his recruits and was responsible to the Squad Sergeant for their turnout. Ours was a nasty little tyrant who was bitter that he had never become an NCO and took it out on us. When he discovered that I had been an actor he never stopped blowing mocking kisses at me and finding unpleasant jobs for me to do.

The routine imposed on us by this monster was frenetic, if not demented. From the moment of reveille he screamed and shouted at us – moving us at the double even while we were washing and shaving. If he thought you were spending too long in the loo he would kick the door open and order you out.

Before going to breakfast we had to lay out all our kit for inspection with fanatical geometrical accuracy. A long piece of string was used to ensure that every last sock and underpant was in line. We then had to 'bump' the floor. The 'bumper' was a heavy instrument wrapped in cloth heavily impregnated with floor polish and on a long broom handle. The floor had to be polished until it shone like a mirror. Then no one was allowed to walk on it! We had to make our way out of the barrack room by easing ourselves along on the horizontal supports of the beds – taking care not to disturb our immacu-lately laid-out kits. After breakfast we used the same method to reach the sides of our beds for Room Inspection. There were times when the Officer treated himself to a lengthy breakfast causing us to have to change from fatigues into Service Dress, including puttees, balancing on the bed-struts so that we would be ready for Drill Parade.

I don't think the Officers had the faintest notion of what was inflicted on the poor wretched recruits by the ludicrously high standards they demanded from the NCOs. Indeed we rarely clapped eyes on our Officers except on the Parade Ground and on Shining Parade.

The latter peculiar Guards institution described a period at the end of the day when we sat on our beds cleaning and polishing all our equipment while the sergeant gave us a lecture on regimental history.

' . . . and you'll bloody remember it when the Officers ask you questions or I'll have your miserable little livers!'

A young Officer would come into the barrack room and carry out an exercise loosely described as 'Man Management'. He would sit as far away from you as possible on the bed while you continued to polish your boots and blanco your belt and ask lots of questions about your family, school and domestic background. Our Officer was a pink-faced youngster straight from Eton and Sandhurst. He apparently thought his experience with the workers on his father's considerable estate had given him 'a way with the men'! He was wrong. The poor boy was completely thrown when I told him in rich tones that I was an actor. His mouth dropped open and he went even pinker as he struggled to say something appropriate before fleeing in confusion to safer ground at the next bed.

The discipline was almost despotic in 1939 and even the most minor lapse would have you in front of the Company Commander at Company Orders. Even having a 'tramline' crease in your trousers could lose you your Name. Losing your Name was having your name taken on Parade. We pressed our trousers by wetting the creases and then sleeping with them under our palliasses. I wasn't very good at it.

'Bond! Look at them bleedin' trousers! Take his Name! Idle while sleeping!'

We soon learnt that it was wiser when facing a charge to accept whatever was dished out. Any attempt to make excuses would automatically double the punishment. For example a rather deaf Major who had been recalled to the Colours was hearing a Charge against a Guardsman Wesley.

'Guardsman Wesley! While on Active Service being Absent Over Leave one hour forty minutes. Anything to say?'

'I thank you, Sir, for leave to speak!'

'Carry on.'

Guardsman Wesley then unwisely told a long rambling story – his bootlace had broken as he was leaving the house causing him to miss his bus to the station – then he couldn't find the RTO to ask for a chit – and so on – and so on. The Company Sergeant-Major was going puce with rage and the Company Commander was straining to hear with his hand cupped behind his ear.

'What's he saying, Sarnt-Major?'

''e says, Sir, that he is a dozy idle man and that 'e wants six Drills!'

A Drill was a harsh minor punishment. The offender had to parade out of his normal duty hours wearing his full equipment, including his big pack loaded with all his clothing and spare boots, his ammunition pouches loaded with weights in lieu of live ammunition which was in short supply in 1939, full webbing, bayonet and his 303 Lee Enfield rifle. The sergeant taking Punishment Parade would then 'chase' the poor unfortunate defaulter round and round the Parade Ground at the quick march, or double, according to his mood. Furthermore, he would give commands in such rapid succession that the wretched man wouldn't know where he was: 'Left TURN! Right TURN! HALT! Quick MARCH! Double MARCH! About TURN! Right TURN!' The slightest mistake would bring forth a stream of abuse and the sergeant would redouble his efforts. On rare occasions when the Duty Officer appeared, the sergeant would temporarily moderate his behaviour. Often men were physically and mentally broken at the end of an hour of a Drill.

My fellow recruits were mainly from working-class backgrounds and physically very strong – but even so they found the pace very demanding. One advantage was that we were all permanently ravenously hungry – hungry enough to wolf down the stodgy, starchy Army food. Those of us who could afford it supplemented our diet with egg, sausage and chips at the NAAFI and countless Mars bars.

It was the first time I had really had anything to do with North Country people and many Guards recruits were from Yorkshire and Northumberland. I had led a pretty protected middle-class existence in the South and at first I found my fellow recruits blunt and a little crude. It didn't take long to discover other qualities such as loyalty and a willingness to 'muck-in' and cover up for any shortcomings in their fellows. They were all volunteers and very splendid men. Some of them realized that I was hopeless at practical things like getting a shine on my boots and brass buttons. They thought I was a bit of a joke and helped cover up for me.

Of course I had had no experience of military life apart from playing 'Raleigh' in *Journey's End* at the Colchester Repertory. I think I subconsciously gave my 'Raleigh' performance on the Parade Ground. I certainly didn't impress our Squad Sergeant but possibly it brought me to the attention of the Company Commander. He sent for me.

'Bond – ever thought of applying for a commission?'

It seemed a most attractive proposition. At least it was a way to escape the hardships of life in the Guards as an Other Rank. What's more I confess that I was a terrible little snob and felt that I truly belonged to the Officer Class.

'Well, Sir, I'd like to try for it!'

'That's the spirit. But you'll have to work damned hard! I'll see you are transferred to a Brigade Squad.'

Brigade Squads were formed specially for Potential Officers. I was in the second one ever formed. This meant that after four weeks of back-breaking Recruit Training I had to go right back to square one and start all over again with the newly formed squad. What is more the Squad Sergeant, one Lance Sergeant Dennis, made it quite clear that he was going to make it hell for us.

'If you lot of bleeders think you're good enough to be Officers you'll have to be the best bleedin' squad ever to pass out – that is if you *do* pass out!'

I think the next couple of months were among the toughest of my five and a half years' service. It was only made tolerable by the spirit that developed among my fellow sufferers.

The majority of the squad were destined for commissions in the Brigade and their backgrounds reflected that. Furthermore they were from all five regiments rather than just from the

Coldstream like my former squad. This caused some complications with the teaching of regimental history at Shining Parade. I had had it drummed into me that the Coldstream Guards' motto 'Nulli Secundus' meant exactly what it said – that the Coldstream were second to none and stood on the left of parade on all occasions because they declined to stand second in line to the Grenadiers who had the arrogance to call themselves The First Regiment of Foot Guards. On any occasion when all five Guards Regiments are on parade the order is – Grenadiers on the Right of the Line, then the Scots, Irish, Welsh and the Coldstream on the left. That is why the white plumes on Grenadier bearskins are on the left and the red plumes on Coldstream bearskins are on the right.

A Grenadier sergeant gave a talk at Shining Parade to the Grenadier recruits. He told them that they were formed from Lord Wentworth's Regiment of Foot – some of whom fled to France with Charles II after the defeat of the Royalist forces by Cromwell. The Coldstream were formed from General Monck's Regiment of Foot. General Monck was captured by Cromwell and imprisoned in the Tower. Then, as the Grenadier sergeant put it: ''e turned bloody traitor, didn't he? He joined the New fucking Model Army under Oliver fucking Cromwell!'

This did not go down at all well with our Lance-Sergeant Dennis who was a Coldstreamer.

''old on! 'old on! Who marched his bleedin' Regiment all the way down from fucking Coldstream in the Borders to put down the riots in London after Cromwell? Who put King fucking Charles II on the throne?'

This was true but General Monck was ordered by the King to march his Regiment to Tower Hill where they laid down their arms in the name of the New Model Army and then took them up again in the name of the King. The Grenadiers, of course, claim that the Coldstream regimental history only legitimately dates from that taking up of arms.

I must confess that this new slant on the regimental history of the Coldstream Guards rather strained my loyalty. As an incurable romantic, I thought of myself as a Cavalier rather than a Roundhead.

My fellow recruits in the Brigade Squad were a very different proposition from my former squad. Like me they were not a very practical bunch, so I had to learn to look after my own kit without help. Some of them, indeed, having led an even more sheltered life than I, found the challenge of the Guards Depot almost beyond them. Institutional food they could cope with, having most of them suffered the hardships of an English public school, but the physical demands made on us pushed some of them to the limit. Iain Moncreiffe, later of that Ilk, in particular, who was not physically very strong, only made it by sheer mental courage – and with some help from the rest of us.

The Trained Soldier was a little over-awed by his new squad but overcame this by detailing anyone with a title to latrine duties. We had two – Hal Astley-Corbett, who was a baronet, and Baron von Hadeln – a refugee from the Baltic. They were given all the dirty jobs which was a great relief because in my former squad they had always fallen to me. The duffer of our squad was one Paddy Leigh Fermor. It took him weeks to learn not to march off with his left leg and left arm. He seemed to be dogged by misfortune and was smothered in Gentian Violet for most of the time as a result of catching scabies from an unfortunate issue of blankets. None of us thought he would make it, but he did. His exploit in Crete when, as a Commando Officer, he captured the German General commanding the garrison was of questionable value to the war effort but was gallantly carried out and after the war was the subject of the film *Ill Met by Moonlight*.

Apart from Baron von Hadeln, there was only one other recruit not destined for the Brigade, Bill Waller, a British Argentinian. He owned a small ranch in La Pampa and on the outbreak of war he rode fifty miles to a neighbour, asked him to look after his affairs, rode back, drove into Buenos Aires, drew every penny he could from his bank, bought a one-way ticket to England and then spent the rest on a glorious binge of wine, women and song until his boat sailed. Like me he had been frustrated by the difficulty in joining up, but for him it was worse because he was broke and had no home in England.

Adrian Pryce-Jones, who was to become a film producer after the war, was a very valuable member of our squad because things became so tough for us that he felt impelled to say something to his father who was a General. He did so very reluctantly and only because Iain Moncreiffe and one or two others were almost becoming physically ill under the pressure Lance Sergeant Dennis put on us. Whatever he said to his father produced results because we began to see a great deal more of the Officers than we had and there was a marked improvement in the supervision of our training.

We were not allowed out of barracks for the first three weeks because we were not thought fit to be seen in public dressed as Guardsmen. When we were finally permitted to walk through the barrack gates on a day pass a group of us hired cars to pick us up and take us to London.

It was very difficult even with a pass to get out of the barrack gates. We had to march, recruit style, swinging our arms up level with our eyes the whole 100 yards from the barrack room to the guardroom and halt with thunderous precision in front of the Regimental Police. The Regimental Police were sadists who tried to find something wrong with your drill or your attire in order to delay you. We wore long blue-grey greatcoats with blancoed webbing belts on the outside. The belt had to be so tight that the Police couldn't get more than two fingers between the belt and the coat. If they could you were sent back to your barrack room to tighten the belt – which meant re-blancoing it and waiting for it to dry – then you tried all over again. It took our car load three attempts before we were all let out.

At Hal Astley-Corbett's suggestion we made for the Cavendish Hotel in Jermyn Street run by the legendary Rosa Lewis. She was a little reluctant to let us in at first but Hal was very persuasive. Rosa Lewis was an extraordinary woman. Her establishment had become a discreet rendezvous for 'members of the gentry' having illicit affairs and King Edward VII and his grandson, later to be Edward VIII, were reputed to have used her facilities. She had, however, a very strict code. If a young officer were to appear with one of the 'tarts' from Jermyn Street in tow he instantly would be shown the door. If, however, he had appeared discreetly with his Commanding Officer's wife he would probably be accommodated. She was extremely generous to us and wouldn't let us pay a penny for anything we had.

'That fat Texan oil man is disgustingly rich. He's paying!'

Most of my fellow recruits in the squad were also quite rich by my standards because I was on a Guardsman's pay of two shillings a day and my savings had diminished buying beer and Mars bars. I had been extremely nervous about how I was going to pay for my share of what turned out to be a pretty wild evening.

Our return to barracks was a hilarious affair. We had the good sense to stop the hired car some little distance from the gates and, realizing we were very drunk, conducted a private drill parade round the corner to sober up. An elderly Captain who had been recalled to the Colours was returning to barracks and observed us with astonishment for a few minutes.

'What the hell's going on?'

We halted in a total shambles and attempted to salute.

'Sorry, Sir, we were . . . sort of practising!'

'You can't fool me. You're all pissed!'

'Well . . . yes, Sir!'

'At least you're honest. Good God! Aren't you Hal Astley-Corbett?'

'Yes, Sir.'

'Thought so – knew your father. How the hell did you get into this state?'

'Been to the Cavendish, Sir.'

'Rosa bloody Lewis, bless her. All right, try to form up in some kind of order and I'll march you through the gates but don't say a bloody word to the Duty Sergeant. Leave that to me.'

Miraculously it worked and we weren't stopped.

Eventually the long-awaited day came when our squad took the square for our final parade. We surpassed ourselves and even Paddy Leigh Fermor marched correctly. As the Commandant left the parade ground the final accolade came from tyrannical Lance Sergeant Dennis: 'I wouldn't bloody well have believed it but *you are now guardsmen*!!'

We all puffed ourselves up with pride – and it was then that the blow fell. The whole squad was to have leave before reporting as Officer Cadets to Sandhurst . . . the whole squad, that is, except Bond, Waller and Baron de Hadeln. The whole of the rest of the squad were candidates for the Foot Guard regiments. We weren't so we were unceremoniously packed off to Pirbright, the Coldstream Guards Training Battalion. It was a shattering blow.

Clearly someone in the Guards hierarchy had a very bad conscience about it because when we arrived at Pirbright Camp our Company Commander sent for us and told us that we were still definitely considered to be Potential Officers and would be given very light duties until room could be found for us at Sandhurst. He kept his word and we had a very cushy few weeks doing practically nothing except going into Woking each evening to have a hot bath and play poker in a friendly pub. It seemed a pretty useless way of spending the war so we were very relieved after about three weeks to be sent belatedly to Sandhurst.

The transformation from the life of a Guardsman to the life of an Officer Cadet at Sandhurst in early 1940 was magical. Each Cadet had his own room with a washbasin and shared a civilian servant with another Cadet. The servant was responsible for cleaning all our equipment, clothing and weaponry although if he failed to do it well enough for the satisfaction of the Staff NCOs it was the Cadet who was given the punishment. We ate in a very civilized mess and were allowed wine at dinner. The only drawback was when the

Staff Captain in charge of your platoon would sit next to you at the table ostensibly to see whether you could handle the cutlery like an Officer. I used to become ridiculously self-conscious on these occasions and start talking as if I had a plum in my mouth.

The training at Sandhurst was much more interesting to me. The square took second place to Map Reading exercises on bicycles, TEWTs, which were Tactical Exercises Without Troops where we would be faced with hypothetical questions from our instructors about deploying our men as if in action, motor-cycle instruction, Anti-Gas training and so on. But I enjoyed the mock battles on Chobham Common and other places above all. These were lovely games of 'make believe' in which I could let my imagination soar. I gave some magnificent performances of personal valour during these mock battles which satisfied my romantic vanity but also commended me to the instructors.

Companies at Sandhurst were organized along infantry battalion lines with three platoons commanded by Staff Captain Instructors and the Company commanded by a Major. Our Company Commander was Major Johnny Goschen of the Grenadiers. He was a charming man and very popular with the Staff and cadets alike. Later in 1944 he was to take command of the Third Battalion, Grenadier Guards at Cassino. After the war he became the 3rd Viscount Goschen.

Most Officer Cadets were riddled with insecurity – especially those of us who had no family military 'back-up'. Having experienced the Guards Depot, and enjoying the comparative luxury of Sandhurst, the thought of being RTU'ed – that is Returned to Unit – was nightmarish. I was extremely nervous, therefore, when Major Goschen asked to see me after his Company Orders one day. What had I done wrong?

'Now, young Bond. Have you had any thoughts about a Regiment yet?'

Of course I had, but there were problems. At that time

every distinguished regiment had a waiting list of possible candidates and without some kind of pull or family influence the chances were slim. There were also the financial problems. Even in early 1940 it was necessary to have a private income to be an Officer in a smart regiment. In my personal situation I had become resigned to accepting whatever posting came up.

'Well . . . no, Sir. I'm afraid I haven't!'

'Leaving it a bit late, aren't you?'

'I know, Sir . . . but . . .'

'How would you like to be a Grenadier?'

I gawped at him in astonishment. My experience after passing out from Caterham had convinced me that to be a Guards Officer was totally outside my reach.

'Of course – you might need a small private income to start with. Do you think you could find that?'

'I could speak to my father, Sir.'

'Why don't you do that? I think you'd make a good Grenadier.'

I went home at the weekend and saw father. I was very conscious of my deal with him over becoming an actor and in my heart I was reluctant to compromise my independence. I needn't have worried. Without hesitation and disguising his pride with some difficulty he promised me £2 a week for as long as I needed it. I reported back to Johnny Goschen.

'Fine! You might find it a bit tight at Windsor or Wellington Barracks but it'll be fine with a Service Battalion.'

Guards Regiments were commanded by a member of the Royal Family and at that time HRH The Duke of Connaught was Colonel of the Grenadiers. However, for all practical purposes the Lieutenant-Colonel of the Regiment was in command. He was Colonel J. A. Prescott who had been wounded in France commanding the First Battalion. He had a formidable presence and my interview to become a Grenadier candidate probably amused him – but it terrified me.

'What makes you think you're good enough to become a Grenadier Officer, young man?'

'I know I'll have to work very hard, Sir.'

'Mm. Well your Company Commander thinks highly of you so far. But you joined up in the Coldstream; what makes you want to be a Grenadier?'

I was inspired.

'Well, Sir, if I become good enough for a commission in the Brigade naturally I'd like to join the FIRST Regiment of Foot.'

'Hum!! Well . . . if you can satisfy the Adjutant, Captain Goulburn, that you're any good – then we'll see!'

Captain E. H. Goulburn, the Adjutant at Sandhurst, was a truly daunting figure. He was, of course, in charge of discipline for the Royal Military College and was held in awe by all Cadets. He was an imposing figure as he took the daily drill parades on horseback and he was the most immaculate officer in the Grenadiers. Later he was to command the First Battalion in Normandy and went on to become Brigade Commander of 8th Infantry Brigade in Holland in October, 1944.

At Sandhurst he was also responsible to Regimental HQ for Cadets who were Grenadier candidates. One evening he asked one or two of us to dinner and gave us a considerable amount to drink. After dinner he plied us with more to drink with our coffee and, having softened us up, proceeded to fire really tough questions at us. I was rather appalled at the sycophancy of my fellow Cadets. When it was my turn he was very rough.

'So, Bond, you were an *actor*! Aren't all actors shits?'

I was so angry that I replied without thinking, 'No more than Regular soldiers, Sir!'

There was a short, tense pause. Then he turned his back on the others and talked theatre to me for the rest of the evening.

At the Guards Depot I had become rather disillusioned by the behaviour of the Officers and the NCOs. At Sandhurst it was a very different matter. All regiments send the pick of their Officers and NCOs to the Royal Military College – perhaps out of long-term self interest? Later in my military career I began to suspect that the Depot became a dumping ground for personnel who were not very popular in Service battalions and not quite bright enough for the Staff.

The senior NCO at Sandhurst was the Regimental Sergeant-Major – RSM 'Bosom' Brand. He was a very big man – both physically and in personality. He was feared and respected by Cadets, NCOs and junior Officers alike. He had built up for himself a reputation for x-ray vision on parade. He did this by the simple ruse of noticing – say – a rifle safety-catch not applied in the third row of a company on parade – say nothing until he was some distance away facing the front rank and then shout: 'That man fourth from the left in the rear rank! Take his name! Idle on parade! Safety-catch not applied!!'

He never tired of his traditional joke when briefing new Cadets.

'You will at all times address your NCO Instructors as Staff! You will address me as – SIR. I will also address you gentlemen as – SIR. Do I make myself clear? You SIR me, Sir and I'll SIR you, Sir. See SIR!'

I was in C Company and our Company Sergeant-Major was a splendid man called Croucher – also a Grenadier. Something about him made him look as if he had stepped straight out of the Victorian era. He was terribly erect as if he had a steel rod inserted up his backside instead of a spine. He had great dignity and I only saw him disconcerted once. Cadets went on parade in alphabetical order and I stood next to Richard Buckle, destined for the Scots Guards. He had joined up straight from Oxford where he had produced a much-praised book of poetry.

One morning CSM Croucher stopped behind him while inspecting us for Adjutant's Parade.

'Mr Buckle, Sir! Get your hair cut! You look like a poet!'

'But Staff! I *am* a poet!'

Croucher's mouth opened and shut like a stranded goldfish and he then moved on without further comment.

In the Spring of 1940 the 'Phoney' war came to an end and, as the German tanks smashed their way through the Low Countries, our training seemed to have much more relevance and urgency. By June, when the Germans forced the British Army into the sea at Dunkirk, morale reached an all-time low. We were given a role in the defence of the Camberley area, but, although it is difficult to believe it now, the whole of the Royal Military College at Sandhurst had only one Bren gun with which to defend itself. Otherwise we only had our First World War Lee Enfield rifles and a very limited amount of 303 ammunition.

I can remember listening to Churchill's famous 'We will fight them on the beaches' speech in the Cadets' Mess. We asked ourselves, 'With *what* are we going to fight them?' That night another Cadet and I got very drunk on port. As I climbed into bed and turned out the light the bed seemed to lift up at the foot and shake very slowly to the right and left. In panic I turned on the light. I knew that if I hadn't I would have been sick and that would have been an RTU offence. For security and economy reasons all lights were turned off at the main at midnight. Frantically I got my bicycle lamp and tied it with string to the overhead light. As it turned round and round I was mesmerized off to sleep to be woken in the morning by a very puzzled servant who looked at the circling bicycle lamp with deep suspicion. Stamping my feet on the parade ground that morning was agonizing.

Towards the end of the course the Adjutant, Eddie Goulburn, sent for me and told me that I had been accepted into the Regiment. At the first opportunity I rushed up to London to order my uniform from Messrs Pegg, who were then the regimental tailors. Regimental Headquarters told us to get our Service Dress caps from Herbert Johnson and our Forage Caps from Lock's in St James's. Forage Caps were blue with gold braid on the peak and looked very splendid, making even the most junior of Guards Officers look like senior Staff Officers.

After Hector Powe, my pre-war 'tailor', I was a little

overawed by Messrs Peggs, Herbert Johnson and Lock's – all by Appointment to His Majesty! Lock's hatshop in particular was daunting. At the first fitting they put a monstrous apparatus on my head with dozens of little bars which they slid in to get the precise contours of my head for the Forage Cap. Looking back I'm convinced that as soon as I had walked out of their shop the hatter said: 'Right! 2nd Lieutenant Bond – a seven and a half bashed out a bit on the left rear!'

The Passing Out Parade at Sandhurst is to this day a moving occasion but in those early days it had a particular poignancy. All taking part were aware that any day they could be in action against the Germans – at that time very possibly in England. Everyone rose to the occasion, especially the Royal Military College Band whose stirring music added to an already charged atmosphere.

Under Eddie Goulburn's confident leadership, our Parade was immaculate and I can remember feeling deeply emotional as, in keeping with tradition, he rode his horse up the steps of the Old Building at the end of the Parade while we hurried off to change into Officers' uniforms for the first time.

Resplendent in my Service Dress, plus-fours and puttees, shining brown boots and crowned by Lock's splendid Forage Cap – I made my way to join my mother and father at the Visitors' Enclosure by the Parade Ground. I passed Company Sergeant-Major Croucher. He threw up a spectacular salute and smiled at me as I fumbled a return.

My father almost crushed my hand with his congratulatory handshake but I found it very difficult to kiss my mother as she was wearing a monumental cartwheel hat which dislodged my Forage Cap. It was a day I shall never forget.

II

The King's Commission

Second-Lieutenants in the Brigade were called Ensigns and Ensigns in the Grenadiers were automatically posted to the Training Battalion at Victoria Barracks in Windsor. To our consternation all new young officers were put on a short drill course before receiving any other training. After the Guards Depot and Sandhurst this seemed to us a total waste of time – and it was.

For days on end we were chased round the square by Regimental Sergeant-Major Robinson. He was a short barrel-like man who had risen to RSM, having joined up when he was sixteen as a Drummer Boy. His most impressive quality was his voice which produced so many decibels that it was claimed that when he was taking a parade in Windsor he could be clearly heard in Slough.

In between drill parades we were given lectures on administration and one very odd lecture which was given to us by Lieutenant F. J. C. Bowes-Lyon. He was a cousin of the Queen and was to collect two Military Crosses in Europe during the last year of the war. His lecture, which he clearly gave with some uneasiness on the orders of the Commandant, was clearly based on the assumption that some or all of us didn't know how to behave like officers and gentlemen.

His lecture pre-dated Nancy Mitford's U and non-U by many years but had more or less the same content. We were told that Guards Officers never wore raincoats – they wore mackintoshes – never 'phoned' but always telephoned – never went 'up to Town' but up to London – never travelled by

Tube or even for that matter by Underground – never carried parcels in the street – never referred to mantelpieces but to chimney-pieces and so on. I don't know who were the most embarrassed – Bowes-Lyon or his audience.

None of this helped my confidence in the Officers' Mess. I was self-conscious enough there in any case. Most of my fellow Ensigns had either been at Eton together or knew each other socially. I was at a great disadvantage and at first I didn't know how to cope. They were all very polite but weren't quite sure of me – rather like the young Officer at Caterham. A common opening gambit from them was: 'Were you at Eton?'

'Er . . . no. No, I wasn't!'

Which put an end to that conversation. It wasn't until a few weeks later that I plucked up the courage to be truthful.

'Were you at Eton?'

'No – I'm an Old Haberdasher!'

For some reason this went down terribly well and I seemed to be accepted socially as a 'bit of a character'. Being an actor, I made the most of it.

At first I was rather over-awed by the older Officers, but an Officers' Mess in the Guards is much more informal than most Line regiments and after a while I found conversation easy and relaxing. Being an actor was a great help here. Many of the older Officers were regular theatre-goers and some of them seemed to envy me.

'Must know lots of pretty girls, mustn't you?'

It was when my contemporaries discussed Officers in Line regiments that I became uneasy. They referred to them as 'Charlie' Officers and I had a nasty feeling that my background could be described as 'Charlie'! Perhaps that was why I spent most of my evenings in Mess with more senior Officers listening with fascination to their regimental stories. Some were clearly apocryphal, some based on truth, but all were fascinating. They gave me an impression of the Brigade of Guards that no regimental histories could ever do.

Before the war the Third Battalion were at Wellington

Barracks and performing London Duties – that is Buckingham Palace and St James's Palace Guard and the Bank of England Picket. A Japanese Major who was the Military Attaché at the Japanese Embassy was a guest of the Battalion for a week. One evening he was sitting alone in a corner of the Mess Ante-Room when a Grenadier Major noticed him.

'Poor little bugger! Nobody talkin' to him! Ought to make him feel a'tome!'

He moved across to the Japanese and towered kindly over him.

'Evenin'! Japanese aren't you?'

The 'poor little bugger' smiled, revealing vast tombstone teeth.

'Yes! Yes! Indeed! Japanese!'

He attempted to rise but the Grenadier thrust him back into his chair and sat beside him.

'Thought so! Haven't you a fella in Japan called Tojo?'

'Yes! General Tojo! Our Plime Minister – very fine man!'

'Of course. You know I had a polo pony once called Tojo. Frightful brute! Had to shoot it!'

Between the wars the young Guards Officers from a battalion performing London Duties were very much in demand during the Season. Subalterns were expected to don white tie and tails nightly and it was very much frowned on by senior officers for them to dine in Mess. Lieutenant-Colonel 'Chico' Leatham, who later became the first Lieutenant-Colonel of the Welsh Guards, very much subscribed to this view and when he observed one of his junior officers dining in night after night, only because he was too poor to be on any debutante's mothers' list and couldn't afford London restaurants, 'Chico' became increasingly irritated. One evening he advanced angrily on the young man who looked petrified.

'Young man! Have you ever had clap?'

'No, Sir!'

'Well – go out and get it!'

When we had satisfied RSM Robinson and Captain P. A. S. Robertson, the Adjutant, that we could move with some precision on the parade ground we moved on to other training. This was extremely disappointing. In spite of the disaster the British Expeditionary Force had suffered from the Nazi blitzkrieg, trench warfare was still being taught at Windsor. A section of First World War trench and a dugout had been built in the Training Area and we spent hours being taught how to revet a trench system by an elderly sergeant.

Battle Drill hadn't been invented at this stage and I suppose with Hitler's troops poised across the Channel it was natural that all the emphasis in our Field Training was placed upon defence. Even so, to a young officer it represented a depressing attitude of mind.

TEWTs, on the other hand, were great fun and our Instructors showed a great deal of imagination. All young Officers would travel out into the Berkshire countryside in a coach – followed by the Mess Sergeant in a 15cwt truck and a three-tonner containing trestle tables and a small marquee. By the time the morning session was over and we broke for luncheon a veritable feast was laid out. There was cold beef, hams – sometimes cold salmon – salads, fruit, Stilton cheese and biscuits. Then, of course, there was the bar presided over by the Mess waiters. Spirits, beer, good wines and port to go with the cheese were available on signature. This was in 1940 when austerity was beginning to bite everywhere in the country – except Victoria Barracks, Windsor!

On one occasion I had made a pig of myself over the port and cheese and was dozing on my feet in the autumn sunshine during the afternoon session when Major Pearson-Gregory, our Instructor, shot a question at me.

'Bond! A mortar bomb has just landed on Company HQ killing your Company Commander. You have now assumed command. Where are you going to deploy your platoons?'

The adrenalin flowed fast – but not fast enough.

'Er . . . There . . . there . . . and there, Sir!'

'Wrong! And you're dead! Now Siddely . . .'

Of course our high standard of living had to be paid for. Our Messing cost us five shillings a day – which was a lot to find out of an Ensign's pay of eleven shillings and sixpence. At one Officers' Mess meeting one young Officer had the temerity to point this out. Lieutenant-Colonel W. S. Pilcher, the Commandant, fell on him like a ton of bricks. He was a very crusty Regular soldier who had some difficulty in disguising his dislike for us wartime soldiers.

'You should count yourself privileged to be in this Mess and it is proper that you contribute to the future of it as well as to the present!'

He referred to the fact that part of our five shillings a day was set aside for re-establishing a proper peacetime Mess after the war.

During his very short reign Edward VIII had built a small airfield at Smith's Lawn in Windsor Great Park. It was decided to keep it in good order in case it was needed in an emergency concerning the Royal Family who spent a lot of time during that period of the war at Windsor. It was very heavily camouflaged with collapsible barns and haystacks made of canvas. These were supported by fine wire cables so that the airfield could be prepared for use in a matter of minutes.

A platoon of Guardsmen was permanently on guard based in an old cricket pavilion used as a guardroom. It was commanded by an Ensign who was billeted in the mews of Cumberland Lodge. I was very excited when my turn came because it was my first command on my own as an Officer. My 48-hour tour happened to fall at a weekend. Viscount Fitzalan and his family were living in the Lodge at that time and I was invited to dinner on the Saturday night. The Duke and Duchess of Beaufort were staying for the weekend and there were a lot of young people with them. We all played Animal Grab after dinner with everyone cheating outrageously.

As I got back to my little mews room I fell into a very deep sleep – fully dressed, of course, in case of an air raid. There was one. The field telephone woke me with a warning of an impending raid and no sooner had I reached my bicycle than enemy aircraft droned overhead. A stick of bombs came whistling down and the noise of the explosions was too close for comfort. I cycled like a man possessed towards the cricket pavilion – completely forgetting the steel wires connected to the camouflage. One caught me smartly under the nose and threw me off. Undaunted I remounted with my nose pouring blood and made it to the pavilion. The Sergeant looked at me with concern.

'Sir! You've been hit!'

'Nosebleed, Sarnt! What's the damage?'

'Couple of the men a bit shaken, Sir, two large craters behind the pavilion and one suspected unexploded bomb!'

I made my report on the telephone to the Barracks and then we started searching for the unexploded bomb hole. It was a pitch black night and we couldn't use strong lights because the raid was still officially on. Soon after dawn the Adjutant rang and seemed very agitated.

'Found that damned bomb yet?'

'No, Sir!'

'Well take the men off searching and get them cleaned up. The King is coming to see the damage!'

'But . . . Sir . . .'

'Never question orders! Get them cleaned up and if they are not immaculate you will be Picquet Officer for a month!'

This was dire threat. The Picquet Officer was what is more usually described as Battalion Orderly Officer – responsible for making inventories of stores, taking Punishment Parades and other boring tasks.

It had been teeming with rain all night and the men were covered in mud from the search. Frantically we cleaned ourselves up and looked fairly smart by the time the King arrived in a large Army Humber with the Commandant and the Adjutant following behind. I gave the order to Present Arms and saluted so energetically that I started my nosebleed again. The Adjutant glared at me and told me to fall out. After inspecting the craters, the King climbed back into his Humber and drove across Smith's Lawn to return to the Castle. The Sergeant and I had just resumed the search when there was an almighty explosion and we were both thrown on our backs. The bomb had gone off directly between the wheel tracks of the King's car. Ten minutes earlier and we would have had Queen Elizabeth II in 1940.

A few weeks later the Officers' Mess had the privilege of entertaining His Majesty to a cocktail party and when, among others, I was presented the King grinned and said, 'Nose all right?'

The most romantic duty for young Ensigns at Windsor was Castle Guard. It remained a Ceremonial Guard throughout the war. A company of Grenadiers under the command of Major G. P. Philipps was stationed in the Royal Mews and was responsible for the safety of the Royal Family who spent a lot of time at the Castle after Dunkirk.

The Castle Guard consisted of a platoon of Guardsmen and was mounted in Victoria Barracks. Then, headed by drums and fife, it marched through the streets of Windsor and up to the Castle. The actor in me loved leading the Guard behind the drums. The men were in battledress but the Officer wore Service Dress with plus fours, puttees and, of course, the Forage Cap.

The Guard wheeled in through Henry VIII's Gateway where the Old Guard were drawn up. There was a short ceremony ending with a fanfare from the Drummer Boys of both Guards as the Officers each took three paces forward and the Key of the Castle was handed over. The Officers then withdrew to the Officers' Guardroom to sign over the Guard and enjoy a glass of sherry while the Sergeants relieved the remaining Old Guard from their posts around the Castle.

The Officers' Guardroom was next door to the Main Guardroom and built into the Castle wall adjoining Henry VIII's Gateway. It was a room of great character with a large open fireplace and very fine panelling. A bed was concealed by an antique screen and the rest of the room looked like a very comfortable sitting room in a country cottage. However, the walls were covered with rather explicit drawings and paintings of women in various stages of undress. Most of them were of great artistic merit and, indeed, one of them painted by a nineteenth-century officer had been framed on the wall. There was also a great deal of witty graffiti and the panelling had names of Officers of the Guard carved over many years. I added my own in a modest position. On the wall by the bed was a very realistic painting of a Victorian Nanny lifting her finger in admonishment with her eyes looking directly at the occupant or occupants of the bed.

I should perhaps explain that Officers were permitted to entertain in the Officers' Guardroom until 8 p.m. in the erroneous belief that nothing untoward was likely to take place at such an early hour.

When in August, 1940, Princess Elizabeth and Princess Margaret expressed a wish to the Commanding Officer that they would like to be invited to tea in the Officers' Guardroom an emergency Mess Meeting was called. What was to be done about the walls? One officer who was puritanical enough to have been a Coldstreamer actually suggested that they should be painted over. He was alone in this view and it was decided that Timothy Tufnell, the Assistant Adjutant, should employ Constance Spry, the florist, to fill the room with flowers strategically arranged to hide the most offensive material. What impression their Royal Highnesses must have gained of Guards Officers' way of living makes one wonder. However, all went well and the Princesses added their signatures which are still there framed above the chimney piece.

Timothy Tufnell and I became good friends and when his mother, a highly successful Estate Agent, was giving a big cocktail party in her house near Ascot Timothy and I wondered how we were going to get there. Since Dunkirk there had been a real crackdown on the use of petrol by the Forces and particularly by civilians. Taxis were non-existent. Timothy had the brilliant idea that we would go on motor-cycle instruction.

An Army Order had been issued that all Officers up to the rank of Brigadier would learn how to ride motor-cycles and Brigadiers and upwards would learn how to ride pillion. This

Order had the effect of filling hospital beds and accelerating promotion.

Timothy and I set out with a sergeant from the Transport Company and raced through Windsor Great Park to the party. Unfortunately we also raced back! We had all three had a very good party and travelled back at an average speed of eighty mph. As we came out of the Park through Queen Anne's Gate and were about to turn into Sheet Street where Victoria Barracks were, I was too fuddled to remember that I was riding a Matchless which had reverse gear-change positions to a Norton which I had been used to. In attempting to change down to reduce speed, I actually re-engaged top gear. I drove slap into a wall. A split second before the impact I raised my hands in horror and fell off. The impetus still carried me into the wall.

The motor-bicycle was a total write-off but I was very lucky indeed to get away with a badly torn muscle in my right leg and the loss of a front tooth which went though my lower lip and broke off. I was carried into the Officers' Mess bleeding profusely from the mouth and a quick-thinking Mess Sergeant brought me a large brandy 'for shock' before the Adjutant arrived and smelt my breath.

After several weeks in hospital I went to a thoroughly incompetent dentist who crowned my tooth without detecting that the root was deeply fractured. One day when I was just about to mount the Castle Guard I thought I detected a slight movement in it. I stood on the square in front of the Guard and RSM Robinson came up to me and gave his highly dramatic salute.

'Castle Guard ready to march off, *Sir*!' I acknowledged his salute and drew myself up to give the commands. I had taken note of the RSM's decibel level and had developed quite a respectable volume myself.

'Castle Guard – *shun*!' My tooth shot out of my mouth on to the Parade Ground. I did a neat Taking Up Arms motion and recovered it before proceeding.

'Cathle Guard – thlope armsth!' I lisped.

The Guardsmen's faces were a picture.

I marched the Guard through the Henry VIII Gateway into the Castle Yard and halted them in front of the Old Guard.

'New Guard! Right Dreth! New Guard! Prethent Armth!'

The Drummer Boys blew the fanfare on their bugles and the Officer of the Old Guard and I took three sharp paces towards each other and he handed me the key. I opened my mouth and revealed my yawning gap. He corpsed.

The Picquet Officer, besides having very boring duties outside the Mess, always took the head of the table at dinner, wearing his Sam Browne belt to signify that he was on duty. The table was adorned with regimental silver from all three regular battalions and looked most impressive. At the end of the meal the Mess waiters took the port round for the first time and then placed the decanter beside the Picquet Officer with a sheet of paper and a pencil. The Mess Waiters then withdrew and each time the port went round the poor wretched young Picquet Officer was expected to keep note of those who helped themselves. At the end of the evening the Mess Sergeant took stock and any missing port was added to the Picquet Officer's mess bill. Some of the more experienced officers were brilliant at masking the decanter with their bodies as they slyly topped up.

Officers were allowed to go up to London at this time, provided they notified the Duty Officer if they were unable to get back before the first parade in the morning due to enemy action. This was quite frequent as the London Blitz had started in earnest. Rosa Lewis at the Cavendish was our favourite rendezvous and she always tried to palm off our bills on some rich civilian because we were 'fighting for your country'. One thing she would rarely do was give any of us a room for the night even if an air-raid was taking place.

One terrible night we had just left the Cavendish and had walked up to Piccadilly in the vain hope of getting a taxi to Waterloo when a major air-raid took place. A stick of bombs fell in the very heart of the West End taking out Montague Burtons opposite St James's Church and setting fire to a large gas main in the middle of Piccadilly. Knowing that the sheets of flame leaping up to the sky might attract follow-up bombing we ran in a circle to the north and then down to Leicester Square. The Café de Paris had had a direct hit by one of the same stick of bombs and the scene was one of carnage. Girls in evening dress and Servicemen in uniform were lying all over the pavement covered in blood. The bomb had fallen straight through a centre well of the building and exploded on the basement dance floor, killing Snake-Hips Johnson and most of his band. It was a sickening sight. We offered to stay and help but were told to leave it to the experts who were there in force and doing a splendid job.

Whenever Waterloo was put out of action by bombing – and it happened often – we had to decide where to stay for the night. A 2nd Lieutenant's pay was only eleven shillings and sixpence a day so it seemed rather extravagant to pay twelve shillings and sixpence for bed and breakfast at the Regent Palace Hotel. The cheaper alternative was the Hammam Turkish Baths in Jermyn Street. The added advantage was that one could sweat any alcohol consumed during the evening out of one's system and have a massage for good measure. It was open all night and in a basement which was a decided advantage during the Blitz. After the treatment and massage one had a cubicle with real linen on the bed and tea and toast served in the morning on real bone china – and all for only seven shillings and sixpence – less than 50 New Pence.

It was every young Officer's ambition to be posted to an active service battalion. I had to wait until April, 1941, before being posted to the Third Battalion in Lincolnshire. Battalion HQ and one company were in Louth and the other three companies were scattered in small towns and villages round the Lincoln Wold. I reported to Lieutenant-Colonel R. B. R. Colvin, the Commanding Officer, and I took an instant liking to him in spite of his opening remark: 'See you were an actor,

Bond! When you've settled in with your platoon you'd better be Entertainments Officer!'

The Adjutant, Captain John Buchanan, was equally charming and he and I were to become good friends over the following months. He told me I was to take over No 4 Platoon in No 2 Company. The Guards always numbered companies rather than lettering them as most other regiments did. No 2 Company was billeted in the small town of Brigg. It was a charming little town and the Company Officers' Mess was in a pleasant suburban house.

The Company Commander was Major S. E. H. Baillie. There was no height standard for Officers in the Brigade but even so I was astonished at how diminutive Simon Baillie was. At six foot three I towered over him. He had sandy hair with a droopy Victorian-looking moustache. He was a difficult man to talk to as he was almost monosyllabic in his speech.

'Bond? Good! Glad! No 4 Platoon! Questions?'

The Second-in-Command was Captain F. J. R. P. Needham who was much more communicative and helpful. My fellow Platoon Commanders were Lieutenant A. K. C. Nation who came from the Channel Islands and Lieutenant D. V. Bendall who had just got married and had his very pretty wife stashed away – quite illegally – somewhere in the town.

At dinner on the night after my arrival I knew at once that I was going to enjoy life much more in a Service Battalion than in the formal regimental atmosphere at Windsor. I also learnt quite a lot about the history of the Third Battalion. It was one of the Regular Battalions and had served with great distinction at Bailleul on the Belgian-French border in May, 1940. It was in this action that Lance-Corporal H. Nicholls was awarded one of the first VCs of the Second World War. Subsequently the Battalion suffered heavy casualties as it played its part in protecting the rear as the British Army retreated to Dunkirk. In spite of that, the survivors marched on to the beaches carrying all their weapons in good order.

The Battalion had been rebuilt and the surviving Officers

and Guardsmen had imparted the spirit and character of the Third to the replacements. I was proud to have joined such a unit.

However, I made a bad start on my first morning when I went to the Platoon to see Breakfasts up. I dressed in Service Dress with plus-fours, puttees and highly polished boots and wore my Forage Cap which I was devoted to. The men's dining room was in the conservatory of the large house in which they were billeted. I tried to conceal my nervousness by leaning negligently on my ash walking stick at the top of the steps leading from the house.

'Any complaints?' My stick skidded on the highly polished marble and I did a spectacular pratt-fall down all three steps. The men loved it. The Company Commander, Simon Baillie, gave me a lecture later, telling me to stick to battledress except on leave.

In the Third Battalion, Parade Ground Drill took second place to Field Training. I enjoyed it enormously and was rather good at it. With aid and encouragement from my splendid Platoon Sergeant, Sergeant Lovett, I soon gained the confidence of my men. Sergeant Lovett was an NCO of the quality that only the Brigade can produce. He was a strict disciplinarian but fair-minded and a very good judge of character. He showed great respect for Officers but recognized my inexperience and was very subtle in his unsparing efforts to put this right. The other NCOs and the men in the Platoon not only respected him but liked him. So did I.

In February, 1941, the First Guards Brigade was to have been the advance guard for an invasion of Sicily – although only the CO, the Adjutant and the Intelligence Officer knew it at the time. The Battalion, together with the Second Cold-stream and the Second Hampshires, had practised assault landings near Inverary on Loch Fyne. Mercifully the plan was abandoned owing to a shortage of troops for the follow-up landing. Such an adventure would have been catastrophically premature at that stage of the war. However, the exercise had done wonders for the morale of the Battalion. There were constant rumours that the Battalion was off on some other adventure and the rumour really took off when in early June, 1941, we were all issued with tropical kit including pith helmets. It was 'reliably' leaked from the cookhouse that we were off to liberate Madagascar! In fact we entrained for Pollock Camp, Glasgow. However, morale soared again when a Marine Commando battalion joined us. The Guardsmen were rather jealous of the Commandos who received additional pay for their skills. The Guardsmen reckoned, not without justification in the Third Battalion, that there was nothing the Commandos could do that they couldn't. There were incidents where the Guardsmen attempted to demonstrate this to the Commandos in the streets of Glasgow with some success – although it didn't go down too well with the Military Police.

We rehearsed two separate landing exercises in June and August of that year, landing from ships in Loch Fyne or off the coast of the Isle of Bute. They were very tough exercises but nobody knew where we were supposed to be going – only that Churchill had personally authorized them. Both were cancelled for reasons which are still secret – but most certainly had nothing to do with the ability of our troops to carry them out.

Pollock Camp was rather a dreary place consisting of Nissen huts built on the site of a proposed Council estate that had been abandoned at the outbreak of war. All the junior Officers were in one hut and our only comic relief was trying to eavesdrop on Rex Whitworth, our Battalion Intelligence Officer, who used to talk in his sleep. We learnt a lot about his sex life but nothing about our military plans.

The Second Hampshires was a splendid battalion which tragically suffered horrendous casualties in their first action in Tunisia. Their boxing team was formidable and when they were about to meet our Battalion team the CO wanted to make sure that it was the best that could be mustered. A Battalion boxing contest was organized and the order given that *all* Officers would appear in the ring. It was decided that the only way this order could be carried out was by having an Officers' Milling Contest. For the uninitiated Milling consisted of two contestants belting away at each other in the ring flat out for three minutes. I had had the misfortune to have taken part in a Milling Contest at the Guards Depot after unwisely confessing that I had boxed at school and was not looking forward to repeating the experience.

I was drawn against Captain Anthony Way and we made a pact not to hurt each other too much! However, once we were in the ring in front of a packed hall of bloodthirsty Guardsmen we realized it was a pact that was impossible to keep. We went at each other hammer and tongs. Lieutenant and Quartermaster 'Fwed' Turner was the referee and he judged me the winner. I had drawn blood from Anthony's nose but he was appalled to see my mouth streaming with blood.

'God! I'm sorry! I've knocked your tooth out!'

'Fwed' then produced my single tooth plate from his pocket and I replaced it and waggled it comfortingly at Tony Way.

'Fwed' was not only a splendid Quartermaster but one of the Regiment's true characters. I shall always remember his famous lecture to young Officers on the subject of Swill. 'Fwed' was quite incapable of pronouncing his R's.

'Now, gentlemen! I'd like to turn your minds to the Scwiptures. Wemember the Sewmon on the Mount? After our Lord addwessed the Multitude he performed the miwacle of the loaves and fishes. He bwoke the bwead and bwoke the fishes and fed the multitude. Then what did He do? Yes – he passed wound baskets to gatha the scwaps! You see – even Our Lowd thought about Swill!!'

After the war he was kept very busy looking after Welfare and Records at Regimental Headquarters in Birdcage Walk.

Colonel Dick Colvin began to worry about the Battalion's morale after so many cancellations following intense training, so he arranged with the Royal Navy for parties to join destroyers escorting convoys through 'E-Boat Alley' between Rosyth Harbour and Sheerness. I took Sergeant Lovett and ten men aboard HMS *Wolsey*, a V and W class destroyer. The men travelled separately and I had been advised by other Officers who had been on earlier trips on no account to join the destroyer the night before sailing. At first I took their advice and went to a hutted transit camp outside the harbour gates. The Mess was full of extremely dull 'Charlies' so I changed my mind and entered the harbour. I didn't know it at the time but my maternal grandfather, John Pennington, who had been a Naval Architect, had designed Rosyth Harbour – and a late nineteenth- century version of the Channel Tunnel into the bargain. I doubt if this valuable information would have been much use to me as I stumbled about in the blackout trying to find the *Wolsey*!

Eventually I discovered her moored fourth out from the quay. I climbed up the gangway of the first ship and saluted the quarterdeck. I was greeted by the Bosun of the Watch.

'The Captain of this ship presents his compliments and invites you to the Wardroom before proceeding to the *Wolsey*.'

In the Wardroom the Ship's Officers made me very much at home and plied the visiting 'Pongo', the Navy's slang word for soldier, with powerful pink gins. After three of these I thought it was time I reported to the *Wolsey* and said so. As I mounted the gangway on to the second ship I noticed that some of the Officers of the first ship were following. I saluted the Quarterdeck and the Bosun of the second ship said: 'Sir! The Captain presents his compliments and would be glad if you joined him in the Wardroom before proceeding to the *Wolsey*.'

Again I was given generous hospitality. The same procedure took place on the third destroyer and by the time I reached the *Wolsey* I was a very happy 'Pongo' indeed. My descent into the Wardroom, I was told later, was nothing short of a major circus feat – however, I was too sloshed to hurt myself. The *Wolsey*'s Wardroom was by then packed with Officers from all four destroyers. It was a conspiracy!

I remember little of the party. I woke up the following

morning in the Captain's Day Cabin as his steward came in with a steaming cup of tea in one hand and a sizzling Alka Seltzer in the other. As I thanked him, I suddenly realized from the movement of the ship that we were at sea.

'God! Have we sailed?'

'Ten minutes ago, Sir!'

I leapt out of bed.

'But my men! I've got to embark my men!'

At that moment Sergeant Lovett knocked and entered the cabin grinning from ear to ear.

'All done, Sir . . . and I've taken the liberty of posting them in positions as required by the Captain, Sir!'

I was rather ashamed of myself and dressed in record time before reporting to the Captain on the bridge. He laughed when he saw me.

'Welcome on board! Your Sergeant is a good chap. Hope you don't mind but I've placed your men where they won't get in the way. Three are in the searchlight tower with a Bren gun and the rest are on the foredeck with their rifles. They can take pot shots at any floating mines we see!'

I was relieved he made no reference to the night before and assumed I hadn't totally disgraced myself. Clearly the whole evening had been a Naval exercise to test the booze capacity of a Guards Officer. The men seemed in good spirits and were clearly enjoying their break from perpetual infantry training. It wasn't to last.

The Guardsmen in the searchlight tower amidships with their Bren gun were eager to be in action against the enemy at last and had been told by the Navy that the chances were pretty good. E-boats were the German equivalent of our Motor Torpedo Boats. They were very fast indeed and were commanded by very daring young German Officers. Apparently they would race into the middle of a convoy, discharge their torpedoes at the merchant ships and then rely on their great speed to escape.

The Guardsmen were to be disappointed. The water was comparatively quiet in the Firth of Forth and the destroyer's speed overcame any rough water but as the *Wolsey* made out into the North Sea it was a very different story. The wind was little short of gale force and as the *Wolsey* manoeuvred to and fro among the convoy like a caring mother duck the ship began to pitch and toss alarmingly. The movement, of course, was greatly exaggerated in the searchlight tower and Guardsmen quickly succumbed. They were so seasick that they would have been lucky to hit the *Queen Mary* with their Bren – let alone an E-Boat. I am a very good sailor and had no problems except timing my movements along the deck to visit the men forward without being showered with vomit from the Bren-gun crew.

It was too rough for the E-Boats so the convoy arrived at Sheerness without incident. We docked in the morning and had a full day to go ashore before we returned to Rosyth on the morning of the following day. I told Sergeant Lovett that if any of the men lived within easy reach of Sheerness they could go home provided they were back in good time. Two of the men were East-Enders and they took all the other Guardsmen home for a 'knees-up'! I joined the Ship's Officers apart from the Officer of the Watch in exploring the pubs of Sheerness. They weren't very exciting but the company was so good it didn't matter. I seem to remember that we filled in the time between 2.30 Closing Time and 6.00 Opening Time by a walk in the country. We came across some donkeys grazing in a field. They were normally used in peacetime to provide holiday rides for children. The sands were now heavily mined and cut off from the land by barbed wire. We rounded them up and set up an impromptu race track. I did very well for the Army because my donkey was so small and my legs were so long I was able to turn my mount into a six-legged beast. The Gipsy owner turned up in a towering rage but was mollified by the generous hire terms we offered him.

The return voyage to Rosyth went uneventfully apart from a successful attempt by Guardsmen on the foredeck to detonate a loose floating mine. It did a lot for the men's morale.

We were sorry to say goodbye to the Navy in Rosyth and

they, on their part, made us feel that we had brightened up what, to them, would have been just another routine convoy duty.

From Rosyth we were all allowed a week's leave before rejoining the Battalion. Leave was always a problem for me. I was terribly torn about where to spend it. During the Summer Season at Clacton-on-Sea in 1939 a young actress called Ann Grace had joined the Company and I had fallen hook, line and sinker in love with her. This rather complicated my relationship with Bob Digby because he had done likewise. I prevailed and when Ann told Bob of her decision he went berserk. In a frenzy he threw himself out of the window of the house we had all rented. Luckily he was too drunk to realize it was a ground floor window and he did himself minimal damage. Ann had returned to her family in Bristol at the outbreak of war and was working with a Government Department that censored Service mail.

I had been astonished to learn that Ann was a widow with a young son of four, Larry. This made no difference towards my feelings about her and during the early months I spent most of my Army leave in Bristol. I became very fond of Larry who had never known his father. His father had died suddenly when Larry was six months old. He had been gassed in the First World War and suffered a severe bronchial attack one night – totally without warning.

My mother, of course, wanted me to spend my leave at home in Farnham Royal where she and father had moved to get away from the Anti-Aircraft Battery that had been installed at the end of our road in the Hampstead Garden Suburb. Many Servicemen had this problem of where to spend leave. It was not unlike the perennial problem of couples – 'Where are we going to spend Christmas?'

In my case love prevailed more often that not and I would make long wartime journeys from Scotland to Bristol, often standing in the corridor for most of the journey. I used to arrive in Bristol exhausted, only to spend nearly every night crouched under the stairs of Ann's house with her parents and Larry. It was their makeshift air-raid shelter and Bristol was a prime bombing target for the Germans.

By comparison, leave at Farnham Royal was quiet and peaceful. I did on one occasion spend a weekend leave in Colchester. Bob Digby and I were back on good terms and were going out for a drink on the Saturday night after Bob had seen the curtain up. I was standing waiting for him on the steps of the Albert Hall resplendent in a long blue greatcoat and Forage Cap when a woman came up to me and for a moment I hoped she would be a pre-war 'fan'. No such luck.

'Are there any two and sixpennies left?'

In the late Summer of 1941 the Battalion had moved to Castle Douglas in Kirkcudbrightshire. It is a delightful market town and the Officers' Mess was in a beautiful eighteenth-century house on the outskirts. Far from us causing any damage to the house, Colonel Dick Colvin saw to it that any tasks that had been neglected because of the war were undertaken by his Guardsmen. My platoon contributed, and at the same time got some practice with their entrenching tools, by restoring the drainage system in the garden and grounds.

Castle Douglas was a dead town on Sunday nights. The pubs and the only cinema were all closed. There was nothing for the men to do and as a result the crime rate increased rapidly. There were silly fights with soldiers from other regiments and somehow some Guardsmen got hold of enough drink to make a nuisance of themselves in the streets. Regimental Sergeant-Major W. Hagell, who became Assistant Chief Constable of England in the 1980s, came to me as Entertainments Officer and begged me to give the men something to occupy their minds and keep them off the streets. Lieutenant Peter Potter, who after the war became a distinguished theatre director, and I had put on one or two Battalion Concerts and Lieutenant 'Boggie' de Rougemont, who was an accomplished jazz musician himself, had got a splendid jazz group together for our dance evenings. All these events made money for our Battalion Entertainment Fund, so

I decided to hire some films for Sunday nights. The cinema owner was delighted to lend his theatre for nothing provided we cleaned it up, hired the films and paid the projectionist. The Town Provost, a strict Presbyterian, did his best to stop us but so long as we didn't charge admission legally he could do nothing about it. We got round this by taking up a collection which was always generous as it was personally supervised by the RSM. I found a very friendly film distributor in Glasgow who only charged me transport and insurance for any films I wanted. I chose some wonderful old films like *The Awful Truth* with Cary Grant and Irene Dunn and *Roman Scandals* with Eddie Cantor.

In one of our concerts four of us, including Peter Potter and John Buchanan, sang Noël Coward's 'The Stately Homes of England'. This was of great satisfaction to me as I had failed dismally when auditioning for it in front of Mr Coward for the original West End production in 1938. Captain Lord John Stanley, now the Earl of Derby, at first took the whole thing personally as he was an 'eldest son who must succeed!', but his sense of humour prevailed. None of the Officers' sense of humour prevailed, however, when a pack of hounds that John Stanley had brought up for a local hunt broke into the Mess kitchens and devoured the entire Officers' Mess meat ration for the week.

Before long the Battalion was off to rehearse for yet another mysterious raid – I now know it would have been an invasion of Pantellaria in the Mediterranean. We embarked on the P & O liner SS *Ettrick* at Gourock and sailed round to Loch Fyne. For a few days we lived like kings as the ship had recently been provisioned abroad and had all sorts of goodies on the menu. This luxury was short-lived as we had to invade the Isle of Bute by jumping into the icy water chest-deep in December. Company HQ and No 4 Platoon were in the same Landing Craft and as the drawbridge lowered Simon Baillie shouted '*Advance*!', stepped forward and totally disappeared from view except for his .38 pistol waving about like a periscope. Once ashore we spent five nights up in the hills, digging slit trenches in the snow and eating iron rations only. There was a group of War Correspondents on board the *Ettrick* attached to Brigade HQ and they were invited to report on our activities. Believe it or not the *Daily Mirror* reporter, who couldn't even be bothered to come ashore with us, acquired a ship's first class menu and wrote an article round it with the headline 'HOW THE GUARDS OFFICERS LIVE WHILE YOU SUFFER RATIONING!'

Once again the plans were abandoned and we returned to Castle Douglas. Anticipating leave, I asked to see the CO. Ann and I had discussed it by letter and we had decided to get married. In the Brigade one had to apply to one's Commanding Officer to do this. I think this dated from the time when rich and titled Guards Officers had a tendency to run off with Gaiety Girls and marry them rather than installing them in riverside bungalows at Maidenhead.

Dick Colvin smiled at me as I went into his office.

'What can I do for you, Derek?'

I took the plunge.

'I'd like your permission to get married, Sir!'

'Good Lord! Who's the lucky young lady?'

'A Mrs Ann D'Eath, Sir.'

'*Mrs*?! I hope she's a widow?'

Divorce was still very much frowned on in the Brigade.

'Oh yes, Sir! He's dead. I mean he died . . . some years ago, Sir.'

'Good! Er . . . I mean – I'm sorry. When is it going to be?'

'I'm not quite sure, Sir, but we might have to get married in rather a hurry!'

'Good . . . *Lord*!'

'No, no, Sir! Nothing like that. It's just that – with all our exercises . . . it's a question really of leave, Sir.'

'Of course, of course! Permission granted – but *do* get it right!'

'Sir!'

I think both of us were glad to bring the interview to a close.

We then got involved in an exercise which involved the whole of Scottish Command and the Free Norwegian Army. The First Guards Brigade weren't taking part because we were now the First Independent Guards Brigade destined for instant derring-dos at Mr Churchill's whim. Instead we provided the umpires. I quite enjoyed this because the white armband worn by umpires gave the wearer enormous powers. You could kill Lt-Colonels and Majors at will. You could wipe out whole units with imaginary enemy firepower. It was rather like being God for the day.

Nigel Nicolson, who had taken over from Rex Whitworth as Intelligence Officer, and I had to report on motor-cycles to the Headquarters of the exercise in Glasgow. We set off at first light from Castle Douglas. It was a very cold day and when we got north of Dalry I saw Nigel, who was leading the way, do the most spectacular Old Fashioned Waltz on his Norton as it hit a patch of ice on the crown of the road. He spun round at least three times but remained on the machine and got it back under control. I slowed down to thirty miles an hour. The next thing I knew I was travelling along the road at that speed on my bottom with no motor-bike! Before I had run out of impetus I had worn through my canvas leggings and my denim fatigue trousers but my long-john underpants were unscathed. I had no way of checking my bum without a mirror. The motor-bicycle was a mess. It was lying in the ditch with the exhaust torn off and the right handlebar at the perpendicular rather than the horizontal. By the time I had dragged it on to the road Nigel had disappeared into the sunrise quite unaware of my plight.

There was no way I could straighten the handlebar but miraculously I was able to start up. The noise without an exhaust was sensational and the steering was very critical with the right handlebar at right angles to the road. By trial and error I discovered that if I could maintain a speed of not less than 35 mph I could keep the engine going. My journey through Glasgow didn't go unnoticed and my arrival at the

Transport Section at HQ was greeted with cheers of derision. I signed for a new motor-cycle and took it to the Station Hotel where I was staying. I bathed and shaved – noticing that my bum was the colour of a blue-assed baboon without the nobs on. It was dinner time so I went into the Malmaison Restaurant and, as I had expected, found Nigel and some other umpires from the Brigade tucking into a splendid meal. Restaurant meals without coupons were supposed to be limited to an upper limit of five shillings worth but provided one used discretion – and cash – one could do much better! We did.

At first light I had to face the long drive from Glasgow to Inverness on wartime roads. I was in agony by the time I arrived, quite unable to sit down. Nigel and I, with two Coldstream Officers, were to be in an umpire pool – we were based on a small pub just outside Lairg. We were there for 48 hours before we were called and we passed the time playing cards and drinking malt whisky. My bum made a full recovery under the anaesthetic of the malt.

I was ordered to sort out a disastrous situation that threatened to wreck the whole major exercise. The Commander of the attacking force from the north and the Commander of the defending force from the south had both unwisely used the Lairg to Tongue road as the main axis of their approaches. It was a single-track road with very few passing places. They had met face to face half-way and the only way to extricate them was to back both convoys out, vehicle by vehicle. It was going to take hours and in the meantime the Norwegians were bowling along the coastal road from Wick to Golspie. My orders were to hold them up for at least an hour at all costs. I intercepted them just north of the bridge at Brora. I stepped into the road in front of the leading Bren-gun carrier.

'You have just been blown up by a mine!'

An enormous Norwegian Colonel with a Viking beard jumped out of the second vehicle.

'Now then, Lieutenant, vat is going on?'

'Your leading vehicle has been knocked out by a mine, Sir!'

'Vat a pity! Such nice men. Never mind. We have now cleared the road and we will continue to advance!'

I could see this was going to be difficult.

'You are under heavy artillery fire!'

'I haf now knocked out the enemy artillery battery with my mortars! We vill proceed!'

I looked round frantically. The bridge!

'Sir! The enemy have blown the bridge!'

'My Sappers are very good, ja? They have builded a Bailey Bridge!'

I knew I was licked!

'Sir! Please, Sir! I just have to hold you up for an hour!'

He threw his arms round my shoulders and laughed up-roariously.

'Vy didn't you say so in the first place. We go and have Aquavit, ja? Is home made! Very good!'

It may not have been a coincidence that the next landing planned for the Brigade on 5 January, 1942, was to have been Norway. It was cancelled because Intelligence revealed that a new German Division had moved near to the place where we were supposed to have landed. Another build-up and let down. It was becoming monotonous.

I took a fortnight's leave on our return from the rehearsal for Norway and went down to Bristol. After three frustrating nights of air-raids, sitting under the stairs with Ann's parents, I suggested that we try to get a Special Licence and marry. I sent a telegram to the Adjutant.

'Getting married 28 January. Request short extension of leave.'

John Buchanan sent one back.

'Seven days' extension granted. Here's to a successful First Night and a Long Run!'

Our witnesses were Squadron Leader 'Mac' Mackenzie, a Spitfire hero who was later shot down and became a POW, and his wife Molly who was Ann's closest friend. After the ceremony performed by a cross-eyed Registrar with halitosis the four of us went to the Grand Hotel for a prolonged luncheon. I pushed the boat out without restraint and was horrified when the bill came to find that I hadn't enough cash and they wouldn't take a cheque – quite common during the war. We had to have a whip-round and Ann and I were only left with enough money to have egg and chips at a cinema café for supper before retiring to bed in our modest hotel. After a visit to the bank in the morning my finances were restored and we went up to Farnham Royal to spend the last few days with my parents. On reflection the whole exercise was selfish and self-indulgent. Both of our mothers were very upset.

Colonel Dick sent for me on my return.

'Congratulations! Don't want to spoil your happiness but I'm afraid it's my duty to tell you that Regimental Head-quarters consider that you got married in a guardsmanlike manner – quite unsuited to an Officer!'

I was shattered. I suppose nothing less than the Guards Chapel and Claridge's would have done! It cheered me up no end to find that Colonel Dick had personally arranged an Officers' Mess wedding present for me. It was in cash and everyone had been most generous.

The Battalion was moved from Castle Douglas to Perth. We were to occupy one half of the Pullars cleaning factory which we were taking over from the Polish Army. I was one of the Officers of the Advance Party and I was horrified to discover that the Poles had dug a twenty-four-seater latrine which discharged straight into the canal serving the cleaning factory. Our Officers' Mess cleaning was handled by Pullars!

In April, 1942, Lt-Colonel Dick Colvin was given command of the 24th Guards Brigade. It was a great blow to the Battalion because he had been a very popular Commanding Officer. His replacement was Lt-Colonel A. S. Hanning. He was a very regimental Officer and he formed the erroneous opinion that the Battalion had become rather sloppy in its drill. Psychologically it was a bad time to stress the parade ground as battle drill had just come into being. It was an imaginative, morale-building method of training which gave every soldier in an infantry platoon an identity and a sense of purpose. The constant drill parades that were called by the new Commander went down like a lead balloon with a battalion that had been so keenly tuned to action over the months.

Luckily at this time another 'prank' was dreamed up in No 10 Downing Street. This time we were to 'liberate' the Isle of Alderney in the Channel Islands. For this we moved down to the Isle of Wight aboard two Dutch cross-Channel ships – the *Emma* and the *Beatrix*. One night we were loaded on to our landing craft with live ammunition and full camouflage make-up for a dress rehearsal. Beaches on the Isle of Wight had been chosen for similarity to the ones we would be assaulting on Alderney. There was a pea-souper fog as we were lowered into the Solent. No 4 Platoon was supposed to be second in a convoy of three craft. The leading one had Company HQ and No 5 Platoon, and No 6 Platoon was in the rear. We were to follow each other in close order. The leading craft disappeared into the Stygian darkness. I turned to the Wavy Navy Sub-Lieutenant in charge of our boat.

'I suppose that's OK? You've got a bearing?'

'Well . . . actually . . . no!'

I could hardly believe it. We had no way of finding our allotted beach. We were hopelessly lost in the Solent. After considerable argument, I managed to persuade our sailor to steer due south in the belief that we were then bound to hit the Isle of Wight somewhere. After what must have seemed like hours to the Guardsmen, most of whom were being seasick, a ship at anchor loomed out of the fog. We were challenged by heavily armed French sailors.

'*Qui va la?*'

For a ghastly moment I thought we had made a one-platoon invasion of France. It turned out to be a Free French Navy vessel. We looked such a villainous crew with our camouflage make-up that it took some time before I could convince the

French crew that we were harmless, that we were lost and that we badly needed to come on board. When the fog lifted in the morning we found we were at anchor a mile off Cowes.

The rehearsal was a complete shambles. Out of twenty-four landing craft involved in the exercise only two made the shore and they were in the wrong place.

At the 'post-mortem' the new Company Commander of No 2 Company, Major K. E. M. Tufnell, came out with some very strong home truths. He had the right because he had had considerable experience of assault landings with the Commandos in North Africa. He had replaced Simon Baillie who had volunteered to join the SAS. Kenny Tufnell was a complete contrast to Simon Baillie. He was well over six foot, had a fierce moustache brushed upwards, wore his Service Dress cap at a very jaunty angle and had his revolver slung on his upper thigh like John Wayne. His view was that the exercise should be abandoned because we just weren't ready. Other senior Officers expressed the same view which prevailed.

All but two companies were sent back to the mainland. No 1 and No 2 Companies were to take part in a raid on a German radar station near Boulogne under the command of Major Algernon Heber-Percy, Second-in-Command of the Battalion. After landing, my platoon was to make the final approach to the radar station and I had to take a small German Jewish Professor with me so that he could identify the piece of equipment our boffins wanted. After the briefing Major Heber-Percy sent for me and told me that under no circumstances was the Professor to be taken prisoner alive.

'Do you mean, Sir, that if things go wrong I have to kill him?'

'What do you think!'

'I think it's terrible, Sir!'

'Not as terrible as the things that would happen to him if he was captured!'

The Professor, who was short and fat, was dressed up as a Guardsman and was referred to as Guardsman Brown. He

1. "I was cast as Prince Charming in *Cinderella*" (p. 7).
Author, centre, bowing to Cinderella; Trevor Howard, far left
as the Demon King. Colchester, Christmas, 1938.

2. "I had no experience of military life apart from
playing 'Raleigh' in *Journey's End*" (p. 17). Author far right.

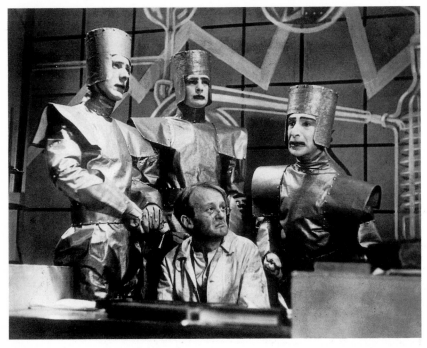

3. Karel Capek's *R.U.R.*, BBC Television, 1938. Author centre rear.

4. *Rope* by Patrick Hamilton. Colchester Repertory company, 1938. Author holding plate; Trevor Howard far right.

was a very nice little chap and the thought of what might happen to him haunted me. Luckily at the very last minute when we were about to board our landing craft the whole raid was cancelled because bad weather had blown up in the Channel. I say 'luckily' because a few weeks later the tragic Dieppe raid took place and I think it likely we might have suffered the same fate. Our ship, the *Emma*, sailed into Southampton and we were all given two weeks' 'disappointment' leave before returning to Perth.

By this time the First Guards Brigade had joined the new 78th Division which had a battle-axe as its Divisional sign. A 78th Divisional Battle School was formed to bring the other brigades up to our highly trained standard and to teach them Battle Drill. Our Brigade was virtually Commando-trained, so had the advantage over the others. I was told that I had been chosen as Demonstration Platoon Commander and the platoon would be formed from young NCOs from the whole Brigade. This was a terrible blow because it meant I would lose No 4 Platoon – my family. I had the gall to ask if I could take my own platoon – pointing out that Officers on the course might argue that they would have to teach Battle Drill to ordinary platoons on return to their battalions – not specially selected NCOs. Major Heber-Percy was to command the Battle School and he grinned when I put it to him.

'Derek, I know perfectly well what you're after! However, if you can convince the Brigadier I'll agree.'

After a good dinner at Brigade HQ I put my case very eloquently to Brigadier Copland-Griffiths and he agreed.

'But you had better not let me down, young man!'

The Battle School was at Callander in the Trossachs – beautiful hilly country ideal for our purposes. Major Heber-Percy had now been promoted to 'local' Lt-Colonel as the Commandant and, after I had installed the platoon in a comfortable little private hotel that had been requisitioned, much to the men's delight, he sent for me.

'Derek, I'm glad you won your battle but you and your platoon have one hell of a task ahead of you. Most of my instructors have come from the Battle School at Barnard Castle and they are going to put you through the toughest training you've ever experienced for the next few weeks before the first course arrives.'

'Put us through it' they certainly did and I knew that the Guardsmen were cursing me for getting them into it.

At the end of our training we were unbelievably fit. Colonel Algy was delighted and gave the platoon what he called a week off. This 'week off' was in fact nothing less than a one-platoon exercise. We marched with full equipment from Callander to Killin and bivouacked in the pouring rain by the side of Loch Tay. Halfway through the week I was invited to a cocktail party by the local Laird – the eccentric Lord Breadalbane.

'Look here, Bond! Have your men been after my salmon?'

'Good heavens no, Sir! Guardsmen don't poach!'

As I returned to the platoon bivouac area – apparently earlier than expected – I smelt a delicious aroma of cooking. Sergeant Lovett hastily interposed himself between me and an enormous bonfire which the men were crowding round.

'Evening – *Sir!*'

In the Grenadiers the word 'Sir' is almost a language of its own. Grenadiers, for instance, are not allowed to say 'Yes, Sir' like lesser regiments – they just have to use a complying inflection on the 'Sir'. There was something about Sergeant Lovett's 'Sir' that sounded remarkably to my trained ears like 'Please bugger off, Sir!'

I returned his salute and brushed him aside. Guardsman Fox, a gipsy, was just removing a second long bricklike piece of clay from the embers of the bonfire and as he broke it open a smell of unbelievably ambrosial beauty filled the air. He had got two enormous salmon, wrapped them in a carefully selected variety of herb leaves, packed them in clay from the loch side and pushed them into the heart of the fire.

'Poached, sarnt?' I asked.

'No – baked, Sir!'

I shall never forget the taste of that salmon.

The first course at the Battle School was made up mainly of Company Commanders from the whole Division. Our job was to lay on a demonstration first thing in the morning and then hand over to the demon instructors who, with absolutely no respect for rank, harried majors and captains ruthlessly for the rest of the day until, if they were still standing, they could more or less emulate our example. My platoon began to forgive me because we were nearly always finished by lunchtime and after the men had cleaned their weapons and equipment the rest of the day and evening was their own.

The Officers' Mess was in a very comfortable Three Star hotel and by the time the Officers on the course had returned, muddy and exhausted, I was to be found lazing in an armchair by the fire, immaculate in my Service Dress and with a large whisky in my hand. I gained the nickname of 'Service Dress Bond'. Fred Majdalany from the Lancashire Fusiliers was the 3″ mortar instructor and he too finished early. We enjoyed talking show business over our whiskies and he was to become a distinguished film critic and novelist after the war.

One of our most spectacular demonstrations was to simulate a platoon attack with live ammunition. The students were lined up between two red flags on a road running along a ridge and while the platoon attacked with live ammunition I gave a commentary. One day Colonel Algy told me I had to lay on a special edition of the demonstration for the Divisional Commander, Major-General V. Evelegh, who was bringing with him a lot of very Top Brass from the War Office. Colonel Algy wanted it to be very frightening and insisted on a trial run of the live ammunition firing. I gave the appropriate orders and bullets cracked past us as we stood between the red flags. I had set all the Bren guns on tripods for safety.

'Feeble!' said Colonel Algy and set off to alter the guns' positions personally. Not satisfied with that, he changed the position of the two-inch mortar as well.

When the Generals and their Staff Officers had assembled between the flags, I began my lecture and waited with trepidation for the platoon to open fire. A hail of bullets whistled overhead and mortar shells exploded far too close. The main telephone wires to the north of Scotland were severed and whip-lashed down amongst the Generals who by now were lying in the ditch shaking with fright. I lay on my back and rapidly fired a red Verey light for the Cease Fire. Colonel Algy took full responsibility. I think he rather enjoyed it.

III

Action in Africa

When all the courses had finished I returned to the Third Battalion with my platoon. Lt-Colonel Arthur Hanning was in his office when I was Picquet Officer one day when Colonel Algy returned from the Battle School and walked into the Orderly Room still wearing his badges of rank as a Lt-Colonel – a rank which had only been local and temporary at the Battle School. He had been told that he was to take over the Battalion but nobody had thought to tell Lt-Colonel Hanning that he was being relieved. It was a highly-charged and embarrassing moment.

The Battalion's morale was considerably boosted by Colonel Algy's appointment as CO and by the time His Majesty the King arrived to inspect us before we departed overseas he was kind enough to tell Colonel Algy that we were the fittest-looking group of men he had ever inspected.

Rumours abounded once more about where we were about to be sent but speculation ended when the news of the 1st Army's invasion of North Africa was released. It was called Operation Torch and the 1st Guards Brigade was to make an opposed landing at Bône and capture the harbour. The opposition was presumably going to come from the French because there were no German forces at that time in Algiers or Tunisia. When the day came for us to entrain from Perth we stocked ourselves up for a very long and uncomfortable wartime train journey – rumour had it – to Liverpool. The Mess Sergeant excelled himself with the amount of food he managed to pack into each individual package.

We didn't need it. Security had been marvellous. In no time at all we were on the quayside at Gourock embarking on a dreadful old Belgian Congo ship called the *Leopoldville*. It had a shallow draft to get up the Congo and even pitched and tossed in the Firth of Clyde. Our convoy went almost to the coast of Greenland in an Atlantic storm before sweeping in a great circle south to the Straits of Gibraltar. At least the weather made it difficult for the U-boats but I have never seen such awful seasickness. Seeing 'meals up' on the men's mess deck could be taken literally. I came across one of my toughest Lance-Sergeants sitting on a bollard on deck looking like one of Dracula's victims.

'Oh Sir! I wish my bleedin' mother had believed in birth control!'

As we moved into the Mediterranean an Officers' final briefing was called. Plans had been changed. Largely because of the conviction the Americans had that the French would fight the British to the death after the sinking by us of the French fleet at Oran to prevent it getting into German hands, the Allied Top Brass got cold feet about our landing in Bône and instead we were to make an unopposed landing in Algiers which had already been secured. History proved this to be an appalling error of judgement. All the evidence now shows that the French would not only not have opposed us but almost certainly would have fought alongside us. It is likely that Tunis could have been taken before the Germans could ferry in any troops and that the Eighth and First Armies could have joined up in Tripolitania in January, 1943, rather than in Tunisia in April.

However, the final briefing for the Third Battalion dealt with more mundane matters. A last kit inspection was to be held the following morning before the men packed their kit for battle. Colonel Algy, knowing the dangers open to men serving in the Middle East apart from facing the enemy, had issued three condoms per man from Regimental Funds. Our Company Commander, Kenny Tufnell, asked a question.

'Are condoms to be shown clean at kit inspection, Sir?'

The landing at Algiers was nerve-wracking as there were several short sharp air-raids as we disembarked and we wasted no time at all getting out of the city which had been badly bombed during the invasion. What the King had described as such a fit battalion had been reduced by sea-sickness to a shambles.

As we marched without a halt for twelve miles, carrying both large and small packs and all our personal weapons plus mortars and anti-tank rifles, there was nearly a mutiny. As we reached the deserted factory in which we were to be billeted near Maison Carré the men were openly cursing and swearing at Officers and NCOs alike. We did nothing about it because there was nothing we could do. In the next few days morale and discipline were restored by the inspired leadership of Colonel Algy and the redoubtable RSM Hagell who magically combined qualities of kindness with an ability to inspire terror into the 'idle'.

We weren't due to move up to Tunisia for a few days and one or two of us discovered that we could buy scent, quite unobtainable at home, and send it by Army post via Gibraltar to our loved ones. One Lieutenant, who enjoyed the name of Johnny Bastard, was quite a ladies' man. Loaded down with scent bottles, he fell off his motor-cycle leaving Maison Carré. He escaped with bruises but his precious scent bottles were all broken and subsequently he led his men into action reeking of Amour-Amour and Jean Patou's Je Reviens!

One day Colonel Algy summoned all the Officers to a conference.

'As we shall be moving up into action in a couple of days I am giving the Officers a last party. All Officers will parade at 1900 hours and transport will take you to the Alletti Hotel in Algiers where I shall send for you!'

When we arrived at the Alletti we only had time for a couple of quick drinks because, as the Americans seemed incapable of holding their drink, a nine o'clock curfew had been imposed. We were in a dire state of drought when at last our Intelligence Officer, Nigel Nicolson – the son of

Harold Nicolson – arrived, having clearly had more than two glasses of wine.

'Follow me, chaps!'

We followed him through the streets of Algiers until we got to the edge of the Casbah. We ended up in a small blind alley which some of us knew could only lead to Le Sphinx which was an Officers' brothel. We surprised a Brigadier who turned bright red when suddenly being confronted with thirty Grenadier Officers.

'Wrong turning!' he mumbled before he fled

Nigel thumped hard on the door. Madame opened the small grill.

'*Nous sommes les Grenadiers. Le Colonel a tout arrangé?*'

Madame opened the door and we sheepishly trooped in. On the ground floor was a large bar and dance floor where patrons could either just drink or dance – or select their girl to take upstairs. The cubicles or rooms were according to the girls' grades. The top floor was reserved for the really high-class tarts who would never be seen on the dance floor but made their appointments either at the Alletti Hotel or by telephone. They were very expensive. We were shown down to the basement where there were '*Chambres d'Exhibition*'. Ours was the largest of these rooms. It had delicate gilt chairs all round the walls for all the world as if we were to be treated to a Brahms and Liszt concert and a very stained divan in the centre with a vast mirror on the ceiling overhead. There were Edwardian wooden coat stands scattered around for any patrons who felt inspired to participate in the proceedings.

There was no sign of Colonel Algy but Nigel had been authorized to order quantities of wine. This was just as well as we were all sober enough to be very self-conscious in these bizarre surroundings. Suddenly the door burst open and Colonel Algy charged in with his hat very much to one side of his head and accompanied by an American General who appeared to have been hit by a bus and a very unsteady civilian who turned out to be a senior official of the new French Government of Algiers.

'Sorry to be late, gentlemen. Now, madame, *cinque femmes s'il vous plait!*'

Why he wanted five we shall never know but the five we got were very much the 'left-overs' from the dance floor. We had all heard the descriptions – 'boopers, droopers and super-droopers'. Our ladies all fell into the last category except one who could well have been a very dissipated choir-boy totally devoid of mammary glands.

After a heated debate round the dreadful divan they started a performance which would have been funny if it had not been so sad. What it certainly wasn't was erotic in the slightest degree. Like most performers who know they are losing their audience their activities became more frantic and bizarre. Their final act was for two to stand with legs wide apart supporting a third on their shoulders while the thin one stood on the shoulders of the fifth and, wearing a dildol which had clearly been damaged in previous use and was stuck together with Elastoplast, proceeded to have simulated sex with the one on the other two's shoulders. This reduced their audience to helpless hysteria. They gave up the battle and, apart from approaching the odd Officer with the invitation 'Suck-suck?', they left us to our drinking. Colonel Algy, who had dozed off, still wearing his hat and clutching his leather stick, suddenly came to and focused on the largest lady who was sitting next to him tossing her breasts in the air one after the other in rather a hopeless way.

'Come on, madam, you're idle! Haven't done anything for five minutes!'

He whacked her across the bottom with his leather swagger stick whereupon she seized it and used it for a purpose for which it was most certainly not intended.

The following day the Battalion had to provide a company which, together with a company from the Coldstream, was to represent the British Army at a rather prematurely named Victory Parade. Major A. C. Huntington commanded the detachment, Captain D. V. Bonsor carried the British flag and I, as senior subaltern on parade, had to give the orders.

Finding a Union Jack in Algiers proved a great difficulty. Nobody had one. The brilliant RSM Hagell was not to be defeated and he approached the Royal Navy who came up with the largest White Ensign they could find. The Union Jack was trimmed out of it and attached to a long mahogany curtain rail. It looked splendid.

The detachment lined up in front of a large Saluting Base built in front of the War Memorial in the centre of Algiers and, as Generals, Admirals and Air Marshals of all the Allied forces appeared, we presented arms.

The political situation in North Africa after the invasion was complicated to say the least. The Americans had rejected General de Gaulle as a possibility to command the French – probably rightly because he was a comparatively junior figure to the military establishment in Algiers. Algiers was then part of Metropolitan France and was the equivalent in military status to Aldershot, Camberley and Salisbury Plain put together. The Americans had extracted General Giraud from Vichy France by submarine, only to find he was not likely to be accepted in North Africa. By chance or design the arch-Pétainist Admiral Darlan was in Algiers at the time of the landing on 8 November. Without consulting their Allies the Americans appointed him Commander-in-Chief. It was a controversial decision about which we knew nothing as we stood in front of the rostrum and saluted, in turn, General Eisenhower, Admiral Darlan, General Giraud and Admiral Cunningham for Britain.

As they all arrived, my head pounding from the Algerian wine consumed at the Sphinx, I yelled my commands in agony. Every arms motion was greeted with applause from the French crowd. One little posse of fans directly in front of me were particularly enthusiastic. I focused on them and saw with horror that they were the girls from the Sphinx dressed in the most outrageous clothes.

''Allo, Lieutenant, 'allo! Good time last night?'

I was so embarrassed I couldn't remember whether my command was at the Slope or Present!

At the end of the parade our reception from the French crowds as we marched ceremonially through Algiers gave the lie to any American worries about the French public's feeling about the British. We were rapturously received and the Guardsmen responded with a splendid display of 'swank' marching. All was well until we returned towards the Saluting Base. A French Chasseur band suddenly struck up 'The British Grenadiers' at a pace that would have defeated even the Rifle Brigade.

The effect on the whole Guards detachment was catastrophic. We minced past the glittering array of Allied leaders like a bunch of poofs!

Before we sailed from the Clyde on 14 November we had heard that some units of the First Army that had landed with the main invasion on 8 November had already reached the borders of Tunisia. There was a feeling of utter frustration in the Battalion because we thought that perhaps we should arrive too late and the First Army would have already linked up with the Eighth Army. Our frustration grew as the days went past at Maison Carré and we had no transport to get us up to the battle. Bône had been heavily bombed and the harbour blocked with sunken shipping. Our troop-carrying lorries were rumoured to be at the bottom of the harbour.

At Sandhurst we had been taught that one of the first priorities in action was to keep the troops informed in order to maintain their morale. Somebody at the top in the First Army had presumably been asleep when that particular lesson was taught when he was a cadet! Colonel Algy did his best but the information passed on to him was sparse. All that he could tell us at this time was that the 36th and 11th Brigades from our 78th Division, together with some armour from the 6th Armoured Division, had crossed into Tunisia. To make matters worse for us the 2nd Hampshires from our 1st Guards Brigade had been sent up to join them. After all our training and all our cancelled operations it seemed to Officers and Guardsmen alike that all we were thought fit for were

Ceremonial Duties such as the Parade in Algiers on 2 December!

The following day, 3 December, to our intense relief and excitement, our transport arrived and lined up among the eucalyptus trees on the road facing east. We had a drive of 500 miles ahead of us and we were told by the Officer in charge of the convoy that he hoped we could make 100 miles a day.

Looking back on it, if only Allied Command hadn't been so nervous about the French reaction to the British and some of the transport available to the Americans in the now vast non-combatant area stretching from Constantine in the east to Casablanca in the west had been sent to our Divisions, we could have been in Tunis by Christmas!

However, it now seemed that the waiting was over and at last the Third Battalion would be back in action against the Germans. It is difficult to describe the importance of this to all of us in the Battalion. Believe it or not, all ranks in the Battalion were longing for action. Over the past months Guardsmen had gone to any lengths to hide any minor injuries or sickness they sustained in case they got left behind. There were no 'skivers' or deserters in our Battalion. In fact the Battalion had embarked at Gourock one Guardsman over strength. He was in my Platoon and he was only sixteen but every inch a Guardsman. His mother had blown the whistle on him just before we embarked by sending a copy of his Birth Certificate to Battalion HQ. The poor boy was shattered at leaving the Platoon. He stowed away on the *Leopoldville* with the active connivance of Sergeant Lovett and the rest of the Platoon. As soon as we were at sea I reported to Colonel Algy that No 4 Platoon was one Guardsman overstrength. He was astonished and at once sent for the 'stowaway'. The boy wasn't overawed by his CO and gave a very good account of himself. Colonel Algy was secretly delighted and agreed that he could remain and be taken back on the strength of No 4! He wrote to the boy's mother and later she withdrew her objections.

The two battalions, the Second Coldstream and Third Grenadiers, embussed on to the troop carriers at dusk. For security reasons and because the RAF hadn't yet had a chance to establish air superiority, we travelled the first leg at night. It was a hazardous business. The troop carriers had to travel with dipped and masked sidelights and no rear light apart from a dim one above the white-painted rear axle. Soon after the enormous convoy set off it was winding its way up the passes of the Lower Atlas Mountains. The road wound in sharp S-bends through dense cork forests growing on the steep slopes. The progress was more vertical than lateral. Tragically one Coldstream vehicle carrying a whole platoon plunged over the side with many casualties.

We travelled on until late morning when we halted and bivouacked round our vehicles among the olive trees. It reminded some of us of a BBC broadcast on 9 November while we were still in Perth.

'Units of the British First Army landed successfully and unopposed in French North Africa yesterday. The soldiers spent their first night in Olive Groves! I'll read that again! They spent their first night in olive groves.'

Olive Groves was one of Ivor Novello's star singers.

The Arabs were very friendly and crowded round us with live chickens held by the feet and tiny eggs which they would sell for Service cigarettes. The children looked like little brown angels with great saucer eyes and gleaming white teeth. Their looks were deceptive as they were the most accomplished little thieves. One Guardsman took off his boots, gaiters and trousers to have a crap behind a bush – carefully taking his rifle with him. Two minutes later he came round the bush. No trousers, no gaiters and no boots!

Our next major halt was at Setif and here an enterprising Arab had set up a mobile brothel which was supervised by the Military Police and a Medical Officer. There was a queue stretching for yards and the girls were regularly examined by the MO. How soldiers could get any kicks out of activities of this kind was utterly beyond me. It was said that some Arab girls would do anything for a spare pair of ammunition boots and the story goes that one Guardsman struck such a deal and when intercourse started he was pleasantly surprised to find that she responded to him by putting both arm round him – then one leg and then the other. He glanced over his shoulders. She was trying on the boots.

We moved by daylight on the next stage and were able to enjoy the breath-taking scenery of the plateau between the Tell Atlas and the main Atlas mountains. The scenery, the Arab villages and settlements, the camels, the exotic smells were both exhilarating and exciting for young men who had mostly never been abroad in their lives. It became a bit too exciting for me when I found a scorpion in my sleeping bag. He missed me but attempted to give my small pack on which I had been resting my head a good old stab with his poison sting.

On the third day we passed through the city of Constantine where 1st Army HQ was based. I had been hoping that we would stop, but apparently HQ was anxious that we should press forward as fast as possible. When we did stop for the night just short of Souk Ahras we learnt the reason why. As we were making ourselves as comfortable as possible in our bivouacks all Company Commanders were sent for by Colonel Algy. They met in a three-tonner with the flaps down as an air raid had been spotted over Bône to the north.

Kenny Tufnell looked very grim as he summoned his platoon commanders, Lieutenants Tony Nation, Bond and Peter Maclean who had taken over from David Bendall, now a Staff Officer away from the Battalion.

'The men are not to be told this but the Hampshires have suffered a disaster!'

Apparently the Hampshires had pushed on as far as Tebourba, only a few miles from Tunis, and were elatedly talking about the possibility of entering the city on the following day when they were attacked by a major German force led by Tiger tanks. The Hampshires fought back gallantly but had no tank support and were overrun. There were stories of the

Tiger tanks running their tracks into the Hampshire slit trenches. When the Hampshires finally withdrew they had been reduced to three Officers and one hundred and seventy men. The full complement for an infantry battalion at that time was 35 officers and 786 men. The Hampshires were no longer an effective fighting force and Brigadier Copland-Griffiths' Brigade had been reduced to our two battalioins.

We were all very shocked as all three battalions had grown very close over the hectic months of training and many personal friendships had grown up.

No wonder 1st Army HQ wanted us to press forward. We were now within range of German Messerschmitts so orders were given to strip back the canvas hoods of the troop carriers and the Guardsmen held rifles and Bren guns at the ready. We were lucky and crossed into Tunisia at Ghardimao on the afternoon of 6 December without attack. We pressed on by night and as we approached Béja we switched all vehicle lights off. There seemed to be total confusion at this point with American light tanks lumbering past in the opposite direction going west.

A Staff Officer thrust his head into Colonel Algy's Humber car which was inching forward at the head of our column and said: 'Thank God you've arrived!'

He then disappeared, giving no explanation or information. We had no alternative but to move slowly forward. I stood on the running board of our vehicle to give our wretched driver some guidance as we could see nothing, even with his nose pressed against the windscreen.

Four miles beyond Béja Colonel Algy made contact with the Brigadier. Apparently the Germans had swept on from Tebourba and were threatening the key town of Medjez el Bab. Medjez hadn't fallen yet but it was very thinly held by the 11th Brigade on a hill called Djebel el Ahmera, later to be known as 'Longstop' and an American force, Combat Command B, consisting of light tanks and half-tracks, who were supposed to be screening the west side of the River Medjerda.

There were strong doubts that Medjez could be held and the Divisional Commander, Major-General Evelegh, had given orders that the 1st Guards Brigade was to dig in on an escarpment at a place called Oued Zaaga on the Béja–Medjez road. We were warned that we must expect all forward units of the First Army to the east of us to retreat through us and we were to hold the position at all costs. Gunfire was now ominously audible so the men set to with their entrenching tools to dig their first slit trenches in Tunisia.

I had always pictured North Africa as sweltering hot with Bedouins careering about on camels. The truth was very different in winter. It was very chilly in the mountains and often pouring with rain. Choosing a good site to dig our slit trenches was quite a problem. The choice was between sodden clay with no lines of fire or lines of fire with outcrops of very hard rock.

What was more, we had no idea what Allied troops were on our right or left flanks, if indeed there were any at all. In theory the 1st Army consisted of the 6th Armoured, the 1st, 46th, 56th, our 78th and 1st Airborne Divisions. To our knowledge at that time only the 78th Division and half of the 6th Armoured were engaged and all the others were in the process of coming up as soon as they could obtain transport. In the meantime we were it! This was when we coined the phrase to parody Churchill: 'Never have so few been commanded by so many!'

No sooner had we achieved the almost impossible task of preparing reasonable defensive positions and placing our weapons when the skies opened. A storm of monumental proportions soaked us all to the skin, turned the tracks into torrents and caused most of the slit trenches to collapse. The Regimental History, written by Nigel Nicolson, who was present, says: 'The Oued Zaaga flood became a legend in the Battalion against which all subsequent discomfort would be measured. It was seldom ever equalled!'

It was a baptism of flood water rather than of fire. Getting food and supplies up to the companies was almost an impossibility. Quartermaster Philpott and RSM Hagell were not to be defeated, however, and with great ingenuity they commandeered dozens of mules from local villages. It was night time before all supplies were delivered. Morale was at rock bottom. A rum issue was ordered and Sergeant Lovett and I stumbled and slid from slit trench to slit trench over our platoon position with a couple of water bottles full of rum. In the Stygian darkness there was no way we could measure out rations so we just let the men have a good swig from the bottles. As a good Guards Officer I took my swig last – thinking there would be very little left. Either the men had shown admirable self-restraint or Sergeant Lovett had been very cautious because I swallowed the equivalent of a quintuple rum in one gulp and became quite happily tight!

One advantage of the storm was that it grounded the German fighters and made it impossible for the Tiger tanks to leave the roads. Medjez, therefore, remained in Allied hands. The Brigadier made a lightning reconnaissance and gave his opinion to Division that Medjez could be held with a smaller perimeter. He suggested one battalion for the station area and another to hold a group of hills to the south-east of the town. The Coldstream were allocated the station area and we were to hold the hills – later to be called Grenadier Hill.

As we fought in the mud to rebuild our positions, drain the slit trenches and dry out weapons and clothing, we were blissfully unaware of this new development. Just as we had completed this almost impossible task we were given the order to abandon our positions and re-embuss on the road. Even the most expressive of Guardsmen ran out of expletives at this.

We didn't have far to go and we made the final approach to Medjez on foot. As we approached the Bailey bridge over the Medjerda River spanning the gap in the Roman bridge which had been blown, we saw American soldiers on foot and unarmed running like hell in the opposite direction. Apparently their General had panicked after two Honey tanks had been taken out by the German Tigers and had given the extraordinary order 'Abandon all vehicles and withdraw on foot!' He was later 'busted' to 2nd Lieutenant. The phrase in common usage in the First Army at that time was 'How Green is My Ally!' I hasten to add that the Americans learnt very quickly, in spite of their inadequate training, and later became first class combat troops.

Medjez was a small market town – more French than Arab – but its strategic importance in war was that it was only twenty miles fom Tunis and lay where the railway and two main roads from Tunis to the west converge to cross the Medjerda River. The Commanders of a scratch French Force of four battalions agreed with our Brigadier that Medjez must be held. They said: 'He who holds Medjez holds Tunis'

Battalion HQ and No 4 Company had already moved across the bridge while we were still struggling out of the mud in Oued Zaaga. Colonel Algy had just been doing a recce at about 8 am in the morning when a column of American armoured cars came speeding down the Tunis road beating a hasty retreat. Expecting the Germans to be in hot pursuit, Colonel Algy and his team of officers scrambled rapidly to a ridge where Captain Tony Way had already deployed No 4 Company round some Arab huts.

Ten German Tiger tanks then appeared on the Tunis road unsupported by infantry. They remained about five hundred yards away wheeling from one side of the road to the other and firing wildly at the whole length of the ridge. It was apparently a Kraftprobe or reconnaissance in strength rather than a major attack. Our troops were not to know that at the time and the mixed bag of Allied defenders let fly with whatever weapons they had. The French had some ancient 75 anti-tank guns, the Guardsmen let fly with their Bren guns and anti-tank rifles – all rather useless against the heavily armoured Tigers. 'Boggie' de Rougement managed to get two of his 3" mortars up and, in a two-hour action, five of the Tigers were knocked out and the rest withdrew. Poor 'Boggie' was killed in this action as a shell exploded by his motor-cycle just as he was about to go back for more mortars and ammunition. He was the Battalion's first casualty.

No 2 Company was given a position on the reverse slope of Grenadier Hill in reserve, while Nos 1, 3 and 4 Companies were on the forward slope. After the Kraftprobe the Guardsmen didn't need any urging to dig in fast. We hadn't many hours of daylight left and the Germans might mount a full attack at any time.

The Guardsmen dug their trenches in pairs but the Platoon Officer and his servant worked as a team digging separate trenches. My servant, Guardsman Woodward, resented the dimensions of my trench because I carried a Lilo air mattress in my big pack and the trench had to be dug to accommodate it. Woodward was a strange man. He was rather a loner and even managed to get a battledress that was a slightly different colour from anyone else's – but not so different that Sergeant Lovett could object. He was a most conscientious servant but rather a poor soldier as it turned out.

No sooner had I blown up my Lilo than I was told to report to Battalion HQ which had been set up in the shaft of an old lead mine running deep into the reverse side of the hill. Getting to it was always a bit worrying as the Germans were overlooking part of the track and would loose off showers of mortars from batteries we called 'Moaning Minnies' whenever they saw anything move. It was a question of leaving one's slit trench very slowly then running like hell until one approached HQ. Then one strolled with nonchalant calm into the cosy safety of the mine.

Colonel Algy briefed me. Apparently three of the five Tiger tanks knocked out in the action were a write-off but the other two only had their tracks blown off. Colonel Algy was in his element to be in action at last.

'Derek! The Bosch are attempting to repair those two Tigers. You're to take out a patrol and blow them up! I've had the Pioneer Sergeant prepare some very powerful gelignite parcels with fifteen-second fuses.'

'Sir! Er . . . Do we have a map, Sir?'

'Map? What the hell do you want a map for? You won't be able to read it in the dark. Don't worry, you'll find it. Pick your own men!'

When I returned to my platoon I made my first mistake in action – one I never repeated.

'I want volunteers for a night patrol straight away.'

After a long pause only two stepped forward. It was a great misjudgement on my part and I knew it.

'Sergeant Lovett – I'll take you and No 3 Section.'

When we got to Battalion HQ, ready to move off, the Pioneer Sergeant was so keen to see his home-made bombs go off that he volunteered to come with us and Colonel Algy gave his permission. We moved off into the darkness in the rough direction of where the Tiger tanks had been seen but it was only after two hours of stumbling about in the dark that we heard a loud and frantic metallic banging. I could see dimmed lights and the German crews repairing their tracks. Their conning-tower guns were fully manned and scanning their perimeter of fire. Moreover, I could see two other Spandau guns mounted on tripods on the ground so that all approaches were well covered. I tried to keep calm when I gave my orders. They were that our one Bren gun was to open fire at an appointed time when the rest of the patrol had made a 'Battle School' approach to the nearest cover to the tanks.

The actor in me enabled me to convey more confidence in the plan as I gave the orders than I truly had! We had just begun to move towards the tanks, my mouth dust dry with fear, when to my intense relief the Germans, having repaired their damaged tracks, climbed aboard and drove off back towards Tunis.

'Right, Sarnt, there's nothing we can do. Back to the battalion!'

'Sir! Don't know about you, Sir, but I think the men could do with a nature halt – know I could!'

'Me too!'

I posted two sentries and the rest of us sat in a row and

dropped our trousers. That was the inglorious end to my first night in action.

Normally when a battalion has established itself in a new position the first step is to liaise with the troops on either flank. The left flank presented no problem. The Coldstream were holding the area of the Railway Station and the Free French were holding the perimeter of Medjez itself. On the right flank, however, there was a gap of at least two miles to the 11th Brigade which consisted of the Lancashire Fusiliers, the Inniskillings and the Royal Ulster Rifles. Liaison was quite impracticable.

To compensate for this junior officers took out night patrols night after night if only to make the Germans think we were thicker on the ground than we were. There was another very practical purpose to the patrols. The vehicles abandoned by the Americans were a potential godsend to the Germans who were flying in troops by the thousand to Tunis but were desperately short of transport – thanks to the Royal Navy which had virtually cut off reinforcements by sea. Our task was to recover as many of the half-tracks and Honey tanks abandoned by the Americans as we could before the Germans got them.

Night after night we went out into the No-Man's-Land between ourselves and the nearest known German positions but the war was so fluid at this stage that neither side really knew where the others were.

Our dress for patrol was very informal to say the least. Each individual devised his own method of carrying what he had to carry. Webbing equipment except belts was discouraged as it was inclined to get caught up in things. We carried ammunition in our battledress pockets. Most of us carried a bayonet on our belts, in my case with the lower part of the scabbard fastened to my thigh with cord. I carried a Tommy gun and in some cases the Guardsmen would as well, instead of their rifles. We never wore steel helmets as the outline of them against a skyline was a dead giveaway. We wore balaclava helmets and blacked our faces.

After a bit one adapted one's training to practical experience, including the necessity on occasions of having to take life personally. One particular recce patrol of myself, one Lance-Corporal and two Guardsmen sticks out in my mind. We were about two miles beyond Grenadier Hill when we suddenly heard the clatter of boots on rock. Before we could freeze we ourselves blundered on to an outcrop of rock. We came face to face with a small German patrol and after a moment of silent shock an unruly mêlée took place. Neither side wanted to open fire and attract attention from any possible main position. It was manual combat. I grappled with a German and used my bayonet with effect. I'm fairly sure I killed him but I shall never know because from some distance a machine-gun opened up and both patrols broke off and fled into the dark. I reproached myself for not at least getting an identification from the German corpse.

It was very unpleasant but we were trained to act rapidly and effectively. There was no emotion or hatred involved. All too often fiction has distorted the reality of personal combat to make dramatic points. There was nothing particularly heroic about it but neither was there anything consciously brutal. Survival was the name of the game.

I realized fairly early on that my servant, Woodward, was highly nervous. I suppose had I been a little older and more experienced I would have tried to have sent him back down the line. As it was I tried to spare him as much as possible and never took him on night patrol. Sergeant Lovett didn't approve of this but I used a rather feeble excuse.

'Must have someone to bring me my tea when I get back from patrol, Sarnt!'

One early morning after a particularly nasty patrol I was dozing happily on my Lilo in my slit trench with the sun on my face and Woodward was halfway between his slit trench and mine with a steaming mug of tea in his hand when a 'stonk' of German mortars came whistling over. Woodward threw the tea over his left shoulder and took a swallow dive on top of me. Every last wisp of wind was expelled from all my bodily apertures but worse than that my precious Lilo burst all its seams. I felt blood trickling on to me and Woodward kept moaning:

'Sir! Oh Sir – my bum!'

Luckily he had only a small scratch from a shell splinter and the demise of my Lilo cheered him up no end.

Our American allies were very honest and realistic about their state of training and requested that some of their Officers should have some battle experience by coming on patrol with us. They were very brave but terribly unfit by comparison with our men so they were something of a liability when on patrol they started puffing and panting and falling behind.

Colonel Algy refused to send them on recce patrols because stealth and silence were essential. For instance the final approach to a German position when the purpose was not to attack but merely acquire information was nerve-wrackingly tense. You slowly extended one hand in front of you and lowered it gently to the ground to make sure there were no trip-wires. Then with the tips of your fingers you gingerly swept the ground of any twigs that might snap noisily and to make sure there were no undetected land-mines. Then very carefully you brought your knee up to the space cleared by your hand then repeated the process with the other hand and the other knee. And then a Guardsman would let rip a thunderous fart!

This actually happened to me one night but fortunately the two German sentries who were within spitting distance each blamed the other and had a good laugh. A conference of Officers was called to discuss what the men were to be fed before going on patrol.

In daytime the Sergeant and I took it in turn to sleep. Although I had lost my Lilo I had had time to enlarge my trench a little and make it more comfortable. When the sun was out my clothes soon dried out after a damp night – on me, of course, because we never knew when there would be some action. This mostly consisted of sporadic mortar attacks, but we also dreaded the American Flying Fortresses on their way back to base after a raid on Tunis because they would often give us a good squirt with any left-over ammunition in their machine-guns. It was not that they were anti-British – just badly briefed and anything that moved that didn't look American they assumed to be the enemy.

Another ally worried us a bit. With the French at Medjez were the Goums. These fierce tribesmen were French Colonial troops from Morocco. The men strolled into action carrying only their rifles. Their wives struggled along behind laden down with their equipment and ammunition. They were superb night-fighters but it was rumoured that they were paid by results. It was said they got so much money for a German ear. Whether other parts of the German anatomy fetched higher prices rumour didn't relate. What worried us was the thought that a German ear must be indistinguishable from a British ear!

Going to the latrine was another worry in daylight. For obvious hygiene reasons the latrines were dug some little distance from our positions and clearly they couldn't have the usual screens erected round them because that would make a splendid practice target for the Germans. To go at all was a momentous decision and choosing the right moment was literally a matter of life and death. There was, of course, the compensation that through nerves the whole operation was very rapid.

Colonel Algy appeared to be totally oblivious of these dangers and would visit the forward troops riding an Arab horse that was so sway-backed his feet touched the ground. He seemed to have a charmed life and the Guardsmen thought the world of him.

Another daytime problem was dealing with groups of Arabs, presumably refugees, who would wander through our minefields apparently under the protection of Allah! We had orders that they were to be searched and if any were found to be in possession of any considerable sums of money they were to be sent back to the French for security checks. The assumption was that they might have been selling information to the enemy. The French were ruthless colonialists in North Africa and we suspected that any Arabs we did send back would very likely be strung up without trial.

I had been told that a good Officer never gives an order he knows will not be carried out and I knew my men well enough to think that they would never send Arab civilians back to their almost certain deaths. I therefore merely searched the Arabs for arms and then released them. Some I searched personally and as a result had the unhappy distinction to be the first Officer in the Battalion to catch lice. Luckily I was able to dispose of them with delousing powder before my Company Commander found out or I would have to have been reported to the Adjutant and I wouldn't have wanted to embarrass John Buchanan!

By this time we must have looked a very scruffy lot. Our second battledresses had all been lost when our supply ship was blown up at Bône. Living in the same clothes day and night for so long must have made us smell of anything but roses.

Our Quartermaster, Lieutenant E. V. Philpott, went back down to Divisional HQ not only to get us some fresh clothing but to raise hell about our rations. In action we lived off compo rations. Each box contained food for seven men for 24 hours. There was tinned meat, soup, vegetables, porridge, condensed milk, tea, sugar, lavatory paper, cigarettes and so on. The boxes varied according to lettering on the outside – A, B, C, etc. The worst box of all was Box X! The main feature of Box X was oxtail consisting almost entirely of bone. The Lines of Communications troops, who rarely saw a shot fired in anger, creamed off all the best boxes leaving us at the sharp end with all the bloody oxtail! The Quartermaster went straight to the Divisional Commander and won his fight. Major-General Evelegh was very much a fighting man's Commander. Henceforth we lived off the best. He also obtained fresh clothing for the whole Battalion.

✳   ✳   ✳

The 17/21st Lancers from the Sixth Armoured Division often made dashing recce patrols almost to the outskirts of Tunis, bringing back invaluable information. The Germans put a stop to this by moving up self-propelled guns to a position near Montarnaud Farm overlooking the main Tunis road some eight miles out of Medjez. Colonel Algy responded to a request for help over this by devising a most unorthodox Battle Patrol to knock the guns out. The patrol was to consist of forty men plus a section of 3″ mortars. It was a most unconventional use of the mortars and the Mortar Officer protested strongly without success.

Colonel Algy put me in command with Joshua Rowley to be second-in-command. After discussion we decided that I would lead with a section from my platoon and twenty men would act as carriers for the mortars and ammunition escorted by another section on the flanks and Joshua would bring up the rear with another section and Lieutenant the Lord Braybrooke, the Mortar Officer.

We moved up in trucks and Bren-gun carriers to the junction of the Medjez–Tunis road and the farm track. We travelled without lights and off-loaded with the greatest caution. It is very hard for forty men to shift such heavy armament about without some degree of noise and we were very conscious of the possibility of German patrols being about. It seemed prudent to me for my section to travel well ahead of the main body because most of the Guardsmen with the mortars and the carrying party had had little experience of night patrolling.

We had been told that the guns we were after were in the general vicinity of Montarnaud Farm – nothing more specific than that and that the French farmer and his wife were still living there and working the farm. I toyed with the idea of asking the farmer to guide us to the guns but decided against it. Some two and a half miles beyond the farm we heard voices and the sound of digging. Corporal Purdue and I moved forward very cautiously until we found a trench freshly dug across the footpath we were following.

We moved a little closer and saw what looked like a Lorried

Infantry Company of Germans digging in all round the guns. Sentries were walking about in a totally relaxed or, as the Guards would describe them, 'idle' manner. Clearly our approach had not been heard. Subsequently it was discovered that these were Panzer Grenadiers from the Hermann Goering Division. Clearly we must take advantage of their vulnerability but there was no way we could launch any kind of general attack with our numbers. I decided to get the mortars as close as possible without being discovered, fire off our whole stock of mortar shells to cause the maximum damage and withdraw hastily.

Joshua brought the mortars up as close as we dared and then I gave the signal to open fire. They did a magnificent job with the mortar barrels almost perpendicular because the range was so short. 130 shells were fired off in less than three minutes.

The Germans were in chaos and taken completely by surprise. At least two vehicles were set on fire but even with the light from the blazing petrol we still couldn't see how much damage we had done to the guns, but we knew we had caused many casualties. As the mortars and the rest of the patrol began to withdraw over the slope behind us the Germans suddenly opened up with Spandaus firing tracer bullets. I realized that I had to cause some diversion to let the patrol get over the hill and out of the line of fire. Besides I thought it might be rather handy to bring back a prisoner so I led my Section in a classic 'Battle Drill' right flanking movement on the nearest Spandau firing tracer. Unfortunately the Germans didn't play by the rules and had what we later got to know as a Silent Section waiting for us. This was a German tactic where they held one Section with a Spandau machine gun in reserve without firing until the enemy were in a position of final attack. Our 'diversion' must have seemed to the Germans to be just that and unhappily we were heading straight for the Silent Section which, of course, we had not been able to pinpoint. They opened fire.

Suddenly I felt as if I had been hit by a sledgehammer in

the left thigh. Apparently I yelled out with surprise and indignation: 'I've been hit!!'

I fell to the ground and immediately Guardsman Pollard, a very brave soldier, jumped up and came to my help. He was killed instantly with a bullet through his back.

Remembering my training, I rolled down the hill, clutching my Tommy gun to my chest, into a wadi – the bed of a dried-up stream. The rest of my Section were already there and two of them had been hit. Corporal Purdue's toes on one foot were badly shot and Guardsman Rigby had the whole of one ankle shattered and was in considerable pain. The Corporal cut off my left trouser-leg and a Tommy-gun magazine fell out of my pouch pocket. After he had put a First Field Dressing on my considerable wound, only partially covering it, he picked up the magazine and showed it to me. A bullet had gone through the guide rib of the magazine and chipped the base of one of the bullets. One millimetre more and I would have been a goner!

By the time Joshua Rowley found us the Germans were putting up flares. There was no point in losing any more men. We had done our job. I gave Joshua the order to take the rest of the patrol and move as fast as they could back to our transport. They were to wait for no more than half-an-hour. If we hadn't appeared by then they were to return to the Battalion. If the three of us couldn't make it that night then we would lie up during the following day and try to make it to the Medjez road the following night. Joshua protested but I was insistent. Like me he realized that the chances of our not being taken prisoner were slim. The flares were getting nearer, so, very reluctantly, he moved off.

As the three of us started to crawl down the wadi I can remember worrying more about the filthy Tunisian mud getting into my wound than any pain. After we had crawled about a mile I had lost so much blood that all I wanted to do was go to sleep. Rigby was barely conscious and was suffering terrible pain. Corporal Purdue took charge.

He decided to see if he could make the farm to get help.

He told us not to move. Not that either of us had the ability to. He then set off hobbling with his wounded toes to cover the one and a half miles to the farm. Both Rigby and I had lost consciousness by the time he returned leading a mule. How he did it I shall never know but somehow he roused us enough to get us on to the beast's back. It was then that I felt real pain for the first time. The poor creature was so underfed that its backbone was like the edge of a saw cutting into my balls.

By the time we reached the farm the Corporal too was very weak from pain – hardly surprising as he had walked about 4½ miles with shattered toes. The farmer and his wife were very tense and nervous and who could blame them with the Germans searching for us so close? The farmer plied us with brandy while his wife ripped up sheets to bandage our wounds and attempted to splint Rigby's foot. Then the farmer lent us a horse and cart driven by a syphilitic Arab with a running, open sore where his nose should have been. As he helped me up into the farmcart his hands touched my bandages. This preyed on my mind for months.

We set off towards the main Medjez–Tunis road at a fast trot, Purdue and I sitting up next to the driver with our Tommy guns at the ready and poor Rigby rolling about in agony in the back as the cart bumped over rocks and ruts.

Just as we were approaching the road we spotted men lying either side of the ditch. The Corporal and I came into the aim.

'Don't shoot. It's us!'

It was Joshua Rowley with Sergeant Lovett and a few Guardsmen who had volunteered to see if they could find us. They had Colonel Algy's Humber car on the road with its engine running and another Guardsman lying on the roof with a Bren gun. Colonel Algy's driver, Lance-Corporal Spreag, always a speed merchant, excelled himself that night. As we reached the the outskirts of Medjez we were nearly shot at by the Free French but we made it back to the Battalion.

While the Medical Officer was cleaning up our wounds I was able to make a full report to Colonel Algy. The relief of being back with the Battalion had got my adrenalin flowing again. We were then put into an ambulance to be driven down to the Advance Dressing Station. Just as the ambulance was about to move off Sergeant Lovett poked his head through the doors.

'Sir! Sorry, Sir, but could I have the Platoon Watch?'

I handed it over.

The Advance Dressing Station was in a small monastery on the westerly outskirts of Medjez. As the orderlies helped me inside hopping on one leg, a doctor asked if I was feeling all right.

'Fine!' I said, and then started to shake from head to foot. Apparently it was a combination of exhaustion and delayed shock. I was given an injection and lost consciousness.

When I came round the whole monastery was shaking with exploding shells and plaster was falling from the ceiling. An orderly was lying on the ground beside my stretcher with his hands over the back of his head.

'Orderly! I think I want a bottle!'

'You'll have to fucking wait — *Sir*!'

This was the beginning of a major problem for me. When I had fully regained consciousness I examined my leg and found it totally encased in plaster from hip to ankle. Penicillin hadn't yet come into use and the method of treating large flesh wounds was to excise all the torn flesh, bullets, shrapnel and muck, then sprinkle the wound with sulphanilamide and immobilize the limb in plaster.

As soon as the shelling was over those of us who had been treated were loaded rapidly on to ambulances and driven off. Still no bottle. At every stop we were given hot sweet tea for shock — but no bottle. Bottles were in very short supply and great demand. If you couldn't perform pretty sharp orderlies would snatch the bottle away from you. At Béja we were loaded on a small local train which shook and rattled its way to the main Casualty Clearing Station at Souk Ahras. By that time I was in agony — not only from the leg which was beginning to throb but mainly from a distended bladder.

There were many casualties at that time and the doctors were worked off their feet. They were sorting out which of the wounded could be evacuated straightaway to Algiers by train and which needed further immediate surgery. It was now three days since I was wounded and I still hadn't had a pee. My stomach was distended like that of an eight-month-pregnant woman. I grabbed hold of a doctor's coat as he was labelling me fit to be entrained.

'Doctor! Doctor, I . . .'

'Don't make a bloody fuss. Yours is only a flesh wound. I've got men with most of their guts hanging out!'

'But, Doctor . . . I haven't peed for three days!'

He felt my bladder.

'Christ! Orderly! Get this man into the theatre straight away!'

I was given a catheter immediately and the Doctor said I was very lucky my bladder hadn't burst. It was weeks before I could pee normally. First it had to be whistling and the pouring of water from a great height then just a great deal of whistling. I found the British Grenadiers the most effective. Later I managed by simply whistling quietly to myself. Apparently it was the after-effect of the delayed shock. Ever since I have had enormous sympathy with sufferers from prostate gland trouble!

The train journey down to Algiers was a nightmare. The Hospital Train consisted of cattle trucks which had been fitted with racks to take three stretchers each side. Sliding doors at each end of the trucks opened straight out to the elements. There was no corridor. The Medical Officer in charge travelled in a very comfortable Pullman at the rear of the train with his French mistress and a plentiful supply of wine. British orderlies were supposed to be supervising the Indo-Chinese orderlies stationed in each truck.

They did no supervising whatsoever but spent all their time brewing tea and tucking into their rations in the Guards Van.

The Indo-Chinese were nice enough but had clearly failed to

master the principles of slipstream. They persistently emptied urine bottles out of the forward sliding door and we spent the entire journey in a fine spray of our own piss.

After some hours of this a Lt-Colonel in the Hampshires who was in the top bunk above me grabbed a British Orderly Sergeant as he was going through and, in spite of a bad head wound, made his authority felt.

'You and your men will supply hot drinks and food to every wounded man on this train within half-an-hour or you will all be in Close Arrest the moment we reach Algiers!'

'Sir . . . I . . .'

'*Move!* . . . and tell your Officer to report to me *at once*!'

The sequel to this journey was that the Officer concerned had to face a Court Martial after a Court of Enquiry had taken evidence from those of us who had travelled on the train.

We arrived in Algiers on Christmas Eve, 1942, and were driven by ambulance to the 98th General Hospital to the west of the city. It was a red brick late nineteenth-century building that had been a French Army hospital. It had only just been taken over and was still in a state of some chaos. Nurses from the Queen Alexandra's Military Nursing Service – affectionately known as the 'Quims' – were on duty and were trying to make some sense of it all. They had just been through a dreadful experience because their transport ship had been sunk in Algiers Harbour with many casualties. This didn't stop them getting straight down to work and their care was quite wonderful.

There had been no little confusion over our rations, so our Christmas Dinner consisted of bully beef sandwiches and cocoa. The nurses did their best to induce the Christmas spirit by singing carols. They sang very sweetly and we were all very deeply moved.

The following day a group of very senior officers from the Royal Army Medical Corps came round and were appalled to hear the stories of the train and see for themselves the conditions in the hospital. They were clearly terrified of

5. "Right!
2nd-Lieutentant Bond
– a seven and a half
bashed out a bit
on the left rear!"
(p. 28).

6. "I had installed the platoon in a comfortable little hotel
that had been requisitioned." (p. 57).

7. "The King ... was kind enough to tell Colonel Algy that we
were the fittest-looking group of men he had ever inspected." (p. 61).
Lt-Colonel Algernon Heber-Percy, Captain K. E. M. Tufnell, H. M. The King.
Extreme right, the author's left hand on ash walking-stick!

8. "Woodward ... even managed to get a battledress that was a slightly
different colour from anyone else's." (p. 75). 4 Platoon HQ.
Woodward centre, rear; the author and Sergeant Lovett in front.

Matron who didn't pull any punches at all. After that things improved considerably.

Among their other problems, the nurses had lost most of their clothing and equipment when their ship sank. They were issued temporarily with Small Men's Gas Impregnated Battle Dress – not the most glamorous of garments. Our Night Sister, a most curvaceous creature who we later nicknamed 'Yum-Yum', wasn't going to put up with this and she got busy with a pair of scissors and needle and cotton to make the awful garment fit in all the right places and her places were very, very right! John Pugh, an officer in the Welsh Guards, had been wounded in the groin and, as a recently married man, was in a great state of anxiety about the future of his marriage. One morning Yum-Yum undulated into the ward and drew the curtains beside John's bed. We heard a joyous cry: 'It's all right!! It's all right!!!'

It was decided to leave my plaster on for the time being as the operating theatre had a long queue of more serious cases to work on. I was able by now to get around on crutches but soon got bored with the confines of the hospital. A Canadian Commando Officer, Prince Paul Lieven, who was the son of a Russian emigré, and I decided to attempt to get down to Algiers. He had part of his right foot blown off and wore plaster from his knee to the foot. He was a brilliant linguist, speaking five languages fluently including, of course, Russian. He was also a most resourceful chap and through a French civilian worker he managed to get hold of a Black Market taxi which ran on a spirit distilled from Algerian wine. Every time it back-fired it smelt like a vinous fart. We recruited two other Officers from our ward to share the exorbitant cost. One was encased in plaster from the top of his head with only his face showing down to the bottom of his rib cage and the other had his right arm in an aeroplane splint. Loading up was quite a problem. Paul got aboard first with his right leg out of the nearside rear window. Then I got in with my plastered leg out of the window behind the driver. The chap with the body plaster then lay across both of us with his head out of the same window as my leg and finally the chap with the aeroplane splint threaded himself in beside the driver with his plastered arm sticking out of the front near-side window.

From behind it must have been a formidable sight and we were cheered and hooted at by every passing vehicle – military or civilian.

Paul's prowess at French helped us to find a Black Market restaurant and, after a splendid meal, we decided to have a nightcap at the Sphinx. Madame greeted us with patriotic fervour!

'*Ah! Les pauvres blessés!* Please – for the blessés all is free!'

All we wanted was a drink, but it seemed churlish to say the least to spurn her offer so we said regretfully that our wounds made anything else impossible. She wouldn't hear of it. Immediately she summoned up some of her more experienced girls who cast professional eyes over us and went into conference to discuss how they could best accommodate our disabilities. While they were still arguing it out we had a swift drink and excused ourselves. Madame looked genuinely disappointed.

My wound by now was becoming very ripe under the plaster and I smelt like an unemptied dustbin. It was decided to remove the plaster and clean me up. For the first time since Medjez I saw the wound. It was quite a hole. The surgeon in charge enjoyed the nickname 'Stitcher' Gibbard for reasons which will become obvious. Apparently he had been a gynaecologist in civilian life and it was a mystery what he was doing in the 98th General. The general theory was that there had been a conference in the War Office discussing the posting of senior medical staff.

'What about this fella Gibbard?'

'Says here he's an expert on wombs, Sir.'

'Wounds? Splendid, send him out to a Field Hospital!'

Gibbard took one look at my wound.

'We'll try stitching it!'

The hole was five inches long and four inches wide. After the operation I was in agony for three days before the Sister realized I wasn't just making a fuss. She removed the dressings. All the stitches had torn their way through my flesh and the wound was gaping wide open again. I had to have another operation to tidy it up.

Sometime in February my Company Commander, Kenny Tufnell, took special leave to come down to see me. He was a very lovable man who never observed the rules unless he thought they served some useful military purpose.

'Got a jeep outside. Why don't you hop in and I'll take you back to the Battalion? The MO can change your dressings every day.'

I undid my bandages and showed him the wound.

'Jesus! What a mess! We all miss you in the Battalion.'

As he was leaving he turned in the doorway and said: 'By the way – Algy has put you up for the Military Cross.'

A few days later I received confirmation and was allowed to put the ribbon up on my battle dress.

Without the plaster I was considerably more mobile and, although I wasn't supposed to, I could walk about with a stick. Paul Lieven and I made regular illicit trips into Algiers. Paul was in financial and domestic problems back in Canada and did not want to be repatriated. He was trying to wangle himself a job with an extraordinary outfit called Allied Head-quarters Psychological Warfare which was based at the Hotel Angleterre. Their purpose appeared to the uninitiated to be to write pamphlets explaining all the Allies to each other and then having their pamphlets translated into German and dropped on the long-suffering enemy.

The Germans, incidentally, were very good at propaganda, as one might expect. One of their most effective pamphlets had a graphic and lewd picture of a GI groping an English girl in a pub car park on one side. The caption was HOW'S THE WIFE, TOMMY? On the other side was a very good dirty joke about an English girl recounting her first meeting with an American soldier:

'You hask 'ave I met any Americans? I'll tell yer! I was coming 'ome from the pub the other night with a pint of beer in a jug for me old Dad when an American sees me, stops me, downs me, ups me, wipes his tallywhacker on me petticoat, swipes the beer, pisses in the jug and walks orf singing "There'll Always Be An England!"'

The Officers on the staff at Psychological Warfare were a 'fragile' lot to say the least. Paul and I had to use enormous restraint as they recounted over dinner the appalling hardships they endured when they first moved into the Hotel Angleterre.

'My dears, it was absolute *torture*! Would you believe that it was *ten days* before we got any decent linen for the beds!'

However, they were an amusing bunch and very kind to us. They had set up a very good cuisine and we dined there as often as we were able to escape the eagle eye of our Ward Sister.

One night Harold Macmillan was sitting at the head table. He spotted the Grenadier Guards regimental flashes on my shoulders and invited us to join him for coffee after dinner. I was astonished to learn that he had commanded No 4 Platoon during the First World War. He was full of questions about how the Battalion was faring. He had been sent by Churchill as a sort of Middle East troubleshooter and he was fascinating to listen to on the whole political scene throughout the area. I shall always regret that I didn't meet him after the war and get him to sign his book *Blast of War*. He was very loyal to Eisenhower, but it was clear from what he said that he thought the Americans at home in the United States had made a dog's breakfast of the North African political scene.

One thing that boosted morale both for the British and the Americans was the appointment of General Alexander to command all Allied Forces in the Middle East. He was immensely respected all round and most people realized that he had planned the strategy of the Alamein battle, while leaving it to Montgomery to carry it out with his jaunty brilliance.

I was becoming very impatient about my wound. It just would not heal. I collared Matron one day and she promised me she would bring a Senior Medical Officer to see it. He took one look at it.

'Skin graft needed. Can't do it out here. Book him on the next hospital ship for England.'

IV

Invalided Home

A few days before the hospital ship was due to leave Algiers an Officer from the Paymaster's Office came into the ward and asked why I hadn't drawn any pay during my stay in hospital. I'd had a very lucky run at poker and in any case there was very little to spend money on. I told him I didn't need any.

'I'd draw the lot if I were you – in francs.'

He then went into such a frenzy of winking that I thought he was afflicted with a nervous tick. However, the penny dropped and I drew all the pay I was allowed from the time I landed in North Africa. It was quite a sum for those days. Just before we embarked, due to pressure from de Gaulle, the franc in North Africa was revalued at 200 to the pound sterling from 300.

The *Oxfordshire* was a Royal Navy hospital ship. It was immaculate and beautifully run as one would expect although the nurses were rather more disciplinarian than our beloved 'Quims'. Once we were clear of Algiers all the lights on the ship were kept on at night and a huge Red Cross was floodlit on the main deck. As we approached the Spanish coast we could see the lights of the Spanish towns to the east and west of Gibraltar ablaze with light. All the walking wounded crowded on to the decks and gazed at this sight in wonder. I thought of Bob Digby and myself standing outside our empty theatre in Clacton with dimmed torches on Friday, 1 September, 1939 – the night the Blackout was imposed in Britain. I hadn't seen towns and cities lit up at night since. It was a very moving sight and made one wonder how much longer the wretched war was to go on.

Our journey through the Bay of Biscay was uneventful apart from a brief inspection by a surfaced U-boat. As we approached Great Britain from the Atlantic I suddenly realized that we were sailing up the Severn estuary towards the port of Bristol. I just couldn't believe my luck. My wife Ann was still living in Bristol and I knew from her letters that she was still working on the Censorship of Service Mail. By a minor miracle Ann had been spared the shock of a telegram when I was wounded.

Just after New Year General 'Boy' Browning, the Airborne Commander, had visited the 98th General during a mission to North Africa to rescue his 1st Airborne Division from being deployed as ordinary infantry. He won his battle and on his way home decided to visit his wounded Paratroopers. I knew he had been a Grenadier so I reached for my battledress by my bedside and put it on over my pyjamas. As he came past my bed he spotted the Grenadier flashes and stopped at my bed. He had served in the 3rd Battalion at one time and was interested to hear news of it. As he turned to leave he said: 'I'm flying home by Gibraltar tonight. If you like to write a brief note to your wife, my ADC will collect it in a few minutes.'

A few days later in Bristol, after Ann had left for her office, my mother-in-law was shocked to get a telegram which merely stated: 'Regret to inform you that your husband, Lt D. W. D. Bond has been wounded in action.'

When my wife returned that evening my mother-in-law thought it wise to let her eat her supper before breaking the news to her. Ann sat at the table and started to open some letters. The first she opened was mine, faithfully posted in England by 'Boy' Browning's ADC. I had said: 'Darling – don't worry but I've had a flesh wound in my thigh – nothing bad but they might send me home!'

As we docked at Bristol I approached the very pompous Lt-Colonel in charge of disembarkation.

95

'Sir. My wife lives here in Bristol. As I'm walking wounded may I go straight home on a short leave?'

'Certainly not! You will go through the proper procedures and entrain to Wolverhampton with all the other wounded! You Guards Officers think you can get away with anything! Typical!'

I was silly to have asked. I should just have walked off the ship, gone home and reported to Regimental Headquarters by telephone. As it was they kept me hanging about in some military hospital in the Midlands for three days before sending me back to Bristol on indefinite leave while waiting my turn for a skin graft. I was to report weekly to the Bristol General Hospital to have the dressing changed.

Some five weeks later I was sitting at the cocktail bar in the Grand Hotel the day before my dressing was due to be changed when a Major in the Royal Army Medical Corps on the next stool gave me a suspicious look.

'Excuse me – but have you trodden in something?'

I told him about my wound.

'Good God! That's preposterous! Look, there's a big American hospital at Frenchay Park with a skin graft unit and no customers. I'll see if I can fiddle you in there!'

He did and within a few days I had a very successful skin graft performed by a Major Bricker who later became one of America's top plastic surgeons. It was a spanking new hospital with quite excellent facilities. It was also manned by the most glamorous Texan nurses. They thought British Officers were 'cute' and their ministrations were very thorough.

Ever since the night I was wounded I had had nightmares about the syphilitic Arab who had touched my wound as he helped me into his cart. Could I have caught syphilis? I had brought it up several times at the 98th General Hospital in Algiers only to be laughed at. I told Major Bricker. He laughed too, but could see that I was anxious.

'No way could you have caught it like that but just in case you've been up to anything your mother wouldn't like – I'll get you a Wasserman test!'

The test was negative and I slept more easily.

While the leg was healing I received a summons to an Investiture at Buckingham Palace. I showed it to Major Bricker.

'Gee! Well I suppose you'll have to go – but take it easy! Stay in an hotel the night before and the night after – walk as little as possible and for Pete's sake come back here immediately the day after! I don't want that graft breaking down!'

I gave him my promise and booked into the Dorchester Hotel for two nights. Ann met me at the station and I was glad of her help because by the time we got to the hotel after a typical wartime train journey my wound was dragging like hell. We had dinner in our room and went to bed early.

It was a very big Investiture. The Royal Navy went in first with about fifty recipients, followed by the Army. There were only four of us and all four were *hors de combat*. The RAF were, of course, the biggest contingent because they operated out of home bases. The Buckingham Palace staff quickly recognized our predicament as we took our place in the line-up for the Investiture and allotted four flunkeys with gilt chairs for us to collapse into as we advanced towards the Monarch.

An Equerry had briefed us thoroughly on how we approached the King. His Majesty was standing on a dais with a ramp leading up to him. When we reached the foot of the ramp we were to be announced by name and rank. We were then to proceed up the ramp, halt in front of the King, turn to face him, bow – then take two paces forward. The King would then talk to us and finally hang our medals on hooks which were pinned in the appropriate place on our uniforms.

When it came to my turn I found the ramp rather difficult with my leg and took an age to get up it. The band had to change tunes before I reached the King and I was acutely conscious that I was making a very sloppy entrance. This was playing on my mind so much that I lost my nerve and got all the instructions wrong. I halted, took two paces forward and *then* bowed. I nearly head-butted His Majesty. The conversation was classic.

'W-which battalion?'

'Third battalion, Sir.'

'F-fine battalion!'

The King glanced towards the ramp.

'H-have you lost your leg?'

'No, Sir.'

'Ah, G-good! My c-cousin has!'

I knew that Captain 'Sandy' Ramsay who was also a Grenadier from the Third Battalion had just lost a leg near Bou Arada and I felt unreasonably guilty that I hadn't!

'I'm so sorry, Sir!'

'Oh, well! Well done!'

My father took the whole family to lunch at the Ivy afterwards and mother, who was glowing with pride and wearing an even more alarming hat than she had worn to my Passing Out Parade, was dying to know what the King had said to me.

'The King seemed to have much more to say to you than the others. What was it?'

'Mother – I don't think I should tell you!'

My leg soon healed enough for me to resume duty but not, alas, with my Battalion as I had been medically down-graded. For the time being I was posted to the Holding Battalion at Wellington Barracks. I was given very few duties apart from the odd lecture to Guardsmen and I thoroughly enjoyed being in London. It was like being on London Duties – without the duties. The Lieutenant-Colonel of the Regiment, still Colonel Prescott, attended one of my lectures and apparently liked what he heard.

I was sent all over the country lecturing at Battle Schools as a supposed expert on night patrolling. I couldn't really think why. The only really valid thing I could say was: 'Don't for God's sake do what I did or you'll get shot!'

My lectures were clearly a success because Regimental Headquarters posted me to the Royal Military College (161

OCTU) at Mons Barracks, Aldershot, as a Staff Captain Platoon Instructor. I joined D Company, commanded by Major Bill Seymour of the Scots Guards. My fellow instructors were Captain Sir Hugh Smiley, Grenadiers, Captain The Earl of Devon, Coldstream, and Captain Sir John Worsley-Taylor, Scots. Perhaps the Commandant thought the Company could do with some leavening from a commoner!

I was thrilled to learn that the job attracted an extra five shillings a day Staff Pay. However, I was extremely nervous about having to teach all manner of things in the curriculum which I had totally dismissed from my mind during my service with the Third Battalion as having no practical purpose in action. I expressed my doubts to Captain Jimmy Whatman, a Grenadier, who I was taking over from. He gave me some excellent advice.

'Your cadets will be far more nervous than you and terribly eager to please. When you have a subject you're shaky on just call up one of the eager beavers – hand him the précis and tell him to give the lecture!'

It worked like a charm.

'Another tip. When you've finished your introductory lecture to a new bunch tell them you'll be available for private interviews afterwards. Then keep a very wary eye on any who come to see you because they clearly lack confidence and are trying to make their mark with you!'

This again was excellent advice as we had only three short months to assess the characters of the cadets. The cadets who stayed behind were invariably insecure. However, there was a notable exception. A cadet called Elliott waited behind at the beginning of his course yet he didn't seem to be the weak or sycophantic type. When we were alone he dropped his bombshell.

'Sir. Before you study my records I feel I ought to tell you that I'm a German!'

I stared at him in disbelief for a moment.

'Well if you've got this far I suppose it must be all right! Tell me the story.'

His real name was Ehrenberg and his father, a Jewish professor, had fled to England from the Nazis before the war. His son had taken the name of Elliott and was a student at Aberdeen University at the outbreak of war. He was arrested as an Enemy Alien and shipped off to the Isle of Man and then to Canada as a detainee. After a year any detainees who were cleared by Intelligence could volunteer to serve in the Pioneer Corps. Elliott volunteered and was soon selected as Officer material. He said he'd like to serve in the infantry and accordingly turned up at the Royal Military College as a cadet.

At the end of the course he walked off with the Belt of Honour. An Enemy Alien!

The Regimental Sergeant Major at 161 (Royal Military College) OCTU was RSM 'Tibby' Britten of the Coldstream Guards. He was a vast man – well over six feet and massively built. His voice was equally large and if RSM Robinson, taking a parade in Windsor, could be heard in Slough, then Britten taking a parade in Aldershot could probably be heard in Farnborough!

He was quite ludicrously 'regimental'. For example in the Orderly Room he always picked up the telephone in his left hand for an incoming call in case it was an Officer on the other end and he could salute the telephone! RSM 'Bosom' Brand, Grenadier Guards, who was still RSM at Sandhurst – now exclusively for Cavalry and Armoured cadets – and Britten were at daggers drawn. 'Bosom' Brand would always omit (Royal Military College) from envelopes he addressed to Mons Barracks, Aldershot, because he claimed that Sandhurst was the only true Royal Military College. Britten hotly denied this and was reported as saying: 'Anyway – real gentlemen don't go driving about in tanks!'

When 'Tibby' Britten challenged 'Bosom' Brand to a Drill Competition between the ATS at Mons and those at Sandhurst the dust really began to fly. First they quarrelled about where it was to take place. Brand won that one and Britten insisted on being allowed to drive the ATS with their 'lady Officers' over to 'recce' the Parade Ground. Then a heatwave started and Britten wanted Shirt-Sleeve Order. Brand fought this and lost but then quibbled about how many inches above the elbow the 'ladies' shirts were to be rolled to and how wide the rolls of the shirt were to be. Both Officers' Messes were hysterical about it and some tried to stir up trouble by suggesting foul play from one or the other of the RSMs.

In the event Sandhurst won and 'Tibby' Britten walked about like a bear with a sore head for weeks. Woe betide any cadet who crossed him at that time!

In the Autumn of 1943 I spent a weekend leave with my parents in Farnham Royal. My father managed to get hold of some Black Market booze and mother gave a cocktail party. Among the guests were one or two theatrical people who lived locally including John Clements, Kay Hammond, Robert McDermot and his wife Diana Morgan who was script-writer at Ealing Studios. I was telling her about Colchester Rep when she suddenly had a brainwave.

'Ealing Studios are having a terrible problem casting young men and they are stuck over their next film *Champagne Charlie*. Why don't you come over and make a film test?'

'I couldn't possibly during the war! Besides, the War Office would never release me!'

'They might. After all you've been in action and been wounded. It's not as if you're a dodger. Even if they don't release you – you'll still have your face on celluloid for after the war.'

This made good sense so I agreed.

The Commandant at Mons was Lt-Colonel Billy Steele from the Coldstream. He was a charming man who suffered badly from a duodenal ulcer. This didn't stop him from applying to return to his Regiment to take over a battalion when he got bored with the Royal Military College! He was highly amused to hear my reason for wanting a morning off.

'All right – but I see you're due to lecture the whole college at 1430 on Platoon in Defence. You'll have to be back for that!'

When the day came the problem was – how to get to Ealing? I worked it out that I could get a train from Aldershot Halt to Surbiton then a number 65 bus to the door of the Studio. My wretched servant forgot my early call. I leapt out of bed, shaved and dressed in record time but realized I could never make the train on foot. The Adjutant's bicycle was leaning against the wall outside the Officers' Mess. I jumped on it and pedalled off like fury. As I reached the station the train was just drawing in. I ran up the steps two at a time with the Adjutant's bicycle aloft over my head and jumped into the Guard's Van. At Surbiton I left the bicycle in the Left Luggage Office and boarded a 65 bus.

I was in good time at the studio. They clapped a period wig on my head, stuck on a pair of sideboards and dressed me in nineteenth century costume. I made passionate romantic love to a very pretty girl in front of the cameras thinking all the time about 1430 hrs and Platoon in Defence. Afterwards I didn't have time for lunch so they packed me into a Black Market hire car with some sandwiches and rushed me back to Aldershot – pausing at Surbiton to tie the Adjutant's bicycle to the roof rack. Back at Mons there was great drama and they were about to set up a Court of Enquiry into the theft.

I got the part and Ealing Studios applied to the War Office for my release. As I suspected this was refused. A few weeks later Margaret Bonner, Ealing's Casting Director, asked me over to luncheon with Michael Balcon. Over coffee he made me an offer.

'How would you like to come under contract to us when you get out of the Army?'

Of course I jumped at it and was taken straight to the Legal Department to have a contract drawn up. I was to get £15 per week when I was demobilized and £3 a week immediately as a retainer 'to help with my Mess Bills'.

Shortly after this I suddenly received a cable from India offering me the job of ADC to R. G. Casey, Governor of Bengal. It came right out of the blue and I was quite astonished. So was Billy Steele when I showed him – and somewhat impressed. He said it was a great opportunity should I think of going into politics or the Diplomatic Corps after the war, but he said I'd have to speak to the Lt-Colonel of the Regiment about it. I was terribly torn, having just signed a film contract, but it seemed too good an opportunity to miss so I went up to Regimental Headquarters at Birdcage Walk.

Within the Brigade of Guards all postings of both Officers and other ranks had to go through Regimental HQ. The Lt-Colonel was furious – not so much with me but with the Governor's Staff for failing to go through the proper channels and applying for me from Regimental Headquarters. However, he also implied that I was behaving rather oddly. He had heard about my film test.

'Not like you, Derek! One moment you want to go off poodle-faking in a film studio. Now you're after a cushy Staff appointment!'

I reacted sharply to this and by doing so sealed my own fate.

'All I want, sir, is to be upgraded medically and return to the Third Battalion!'

'Good man!'

As I made my way back to Aldershot I began to think that I had made one of the worst mistakes of my life and I have often wondered what different course my life might have taken had I gone to India.

Very soon after this the Lt-Colonel put me in charge of the Grenadier intake of cadets. I took it as a great honour and I was very tough with my charges – taking a page out of Eddie Goulburn's book!

Over the years I have met many of my former cadets, including Kenneth Kendall, the BBC news reader. Apparently I was thought to be a bit of a softy in the lecture room but a tyrant on Field Training. I think this was probably true because I was very conscious of the fact that soon after the cadets were commissioned they would find themselves in action and responsible for the lives of their command. This was very much in all instructors' minds in 1944 with D-Day in the offing.

I devised one little exercise to make the cadets think quickly under stress about the use of the weapons they had at their command. I provided the stress and the cadets had to do the thinking. In the course of the exercise a section had to cross a gap in cover along a hedge. It was so abundantly clear that a phosphorus smoke grenade should be used that when a cadet acting as section leader just lay there with his mouth open – I lost my temper. 'Think, man, think. Don't just fucking lie there! *Do something!*'

He did something all right. In panic he hurled a phosphoros grenade without taking proper aim. It hit a tree above my head, exploded and set me on fire from head to foot. I ran like hell stripping off my burning clothing as I went – followed by all my cadets yelling at me. They thought I had lost my head. In fact I was heading for a stagnant pool which I plunged into to extinguish myself. Keeping my soaking shirt over my face I was rushed off to the Cambridge Hospital. I knew that phosphorus would ignite if exposed to the air and my face was covered in fragments. A young doctor spent two hours picking out the pieces and I ended up totally bandaged except for my eyes and mouth. The doctor told me that I might be lucky and get away with superficial burns at the best or be a skin graft case at the worst. I wouldn't know for four days when they would remove the bandages. So much for Ealing Studios, I thought.

On the second day the cadet responsible came to see me. The poor man was terribly on edge.

'Sir? Will this affect my chances of getting a Commission?'

I muttered through my bandages: 'That fucking stupid question will!'

I was lucky. No scarring – only a tendency to have rather a ruddy complexion when I'm not suntanned.

The interview I had had with the Lt-Colonel over the India business played on my mind. I had said that I wanted to rejoin the Third Battalion out of self-defence but now I began to realize that I really meant it. I was getting very tired of lecturing. However, the first problem was to get put back up to A1 medically. I had met the Lt-Colonel in charge of the Standing Medical Board in Aldershot when he had been a guest in our Mess. I remembered that he was an even worse snob than I was so I decided to work on him. I recruited my three brother officers – Hugh Smiley, John Worsley-Taylor, and – my ace in the hole – Christopher Devon. We all got on very well and were renowned for a certain amount of hell-raising in the Mess. The four of us took the doctor out to dinner and then on to the Aldershot Hippodrome to see Phyllis Dixey, the Strip Tease Queen. She was a superb artist uniquely combining sexiness with purity and innocence. Her husband, Dick Tracey, was a down-to-earth vulgar comic. At the end of his act a song sheet came down and he made us all sing. We were sitting in a box, clearly pre-arranged by the Manager. A spotlight was flashed on to us.

'And now – we'll have the CO and his gang!'

The lyric was:

> Susy! Susy! Sitting in a Shoe Shine Shop
> All day long She Sits and Shines
> All day long She Shines and Sits
> She Sits and Shines and Shines and Sits
> Sitting in a Shoe Shine Shop!

As the orchestra speeded up inevitably we were 'Shitting' all over the place!

The evening was a huge success and a few days later a special Medical Board put me back up to A1.

One of the night exercises we had devised for the cadets towards the end of their course was called Company in Defence. Hugh Smiley had persuaded our Company Commander, Bill Seymour, that his own house on a small hillock near the Hog's Back in Surrey was an ideal location for the exercise. Hugh's wife, Nancy, Cecil Beaton's sister, was a superb cook. As my departure from the RMC was imminent it was decided to give me a farewell dinner party. Once we had got the cadets digging themselves in all round the house, incidentally in the pouring rain, we adjourned to the drawing room for drinks before dinner. It was a hilarious evening, although we did have to take it in turn to 'supervise' the cadets.

My last course finished towards the end of May, 1944, and I felt rather sad on the Passing Out Parade as the Adjutant rode his horse up the steps at the end of the Parade. That tradition was kept up at Mons Barracks although the steps only led to a path rather than into the Old Building as they did at Sandhurst.

The cadets at that stage of the war came from a much broader background than they had in 1940. I think this caused some family problems for them. This became rather apparent at the Passing Out Parade. After the cadets had changed into Officer's uniform for the first time I used to wait near the families to say good bye to them. The cadets that came up to me and said: 'Sir – I'd like you to meet me Mum!' were clearly going to be all right. Some others, I'm afraid, tried to smuggle the Mum/wife/girlfriend away without introduction and this used to trouble me. I often wondered what effect their change in status would have on their family lives in the long term.

After a week's leave I was posted to Windsor to await my posting back to the Third Battalion. Lt-Colonel G. M. Cornish ('Billikin' Cornish) had taken over from Colonel Pilcher as Commandant. He had commanded the Second Battalion at the outbreak of war until the end of April, 1940. Whether or not it was due to his more relaxed attitude to junior Officers, the atmosphere in the Mess was much more congenial than I remembered it in 1940. It could have been that I was now totally at ease in the Mess and I was, after all, a Captain with battle experience. Remembering how I felt when I had first joined, I went out of my way to talk to the new young Officers, some of whom had been my cadets. One of the nicest conventions in a Grenadier Officers' Mess was that all Officers irrespective of rank addressed each other by surnames only until the senior Officer used a junior Officer's Christian name.

The junior Officer could then use the senior Officer's Christian name. Officers' ranks were never used in the Mess and only the Commanding Officer was called 'Sir'.

One very odd custom which I used at times was that an Officer could wear his cap at breakfast. If he did it signified to other Officers that he was not to be addressed under any circumstances. When I was an Ensign I had made the mistake of asking James Bowes-Lyon to pass the marmalade when he was wearing his cap. I received a withering look and no marmalade.

At the end of May, 1944, we had a riotous farewell party for Viscount Lascelles who was off to join the Third Battalion. As we poured him on to the train at Windsor and Eton Station I made him promise to warn them that I was on my way back to join them. A month later he was wounded at Perugia and taken prisoner.

V

Reunion in Italy

In mid-July Regimental Headquarters used its influence to have me flown out to Italy via Gibraltar and Algiers. I had never flown before and I was very excited by it. In the event it was almost too exciting. For security reasons we took off at night from an airfield in Cornwall. It was a transport plane with no seating apart from the metal benches along the sides of the cabin. There were six Army Officers of varying ranks and Air Vice Marshal de Bescombe. We were warned there was no heating so we wrapped ourselves in blankets and attempted to get some sleep on the floor. It was a long flight as we had to fly round the Spanish coast well outside territorial waters. At dawn as we approached Gibraltar the pilot came into the cabin and spoke to the Air Vice Marshal.

'Sorry, Sir. La Linea is fog-bound, so we've been diverted to North Africa!'

'Fuel?'

'Tight, Sir, but we should make it.'

Half an hour later he came back into the cabin.

'Sorry, Sir. Oran is fog-bound too! We'll have to return to La Linea.'

'Fuel?'

'Low, Sir. This time we'll just have to land – but it'll be rough!'

I was beginning to wish we hadn't got an Air Vice Marshal with us. Ignorance is bliss. He turned to us, white-faced, and said: 'Now listen carefully! As we come in to land sit like this and put your arms through the struts like this . . . and pray!'

We overshot on our first attempt and as the plane revved and banked it seemed that our wheels almost touched the Rock as it loomed out of the fog. On the second attempt we made it but had to leapfrog over the wreckage of a York transport that had belly-flopped on the edge of the runway just a little earlier, severely injuring all on board.

Those of us going on to Algiers were told we had a couple of hours to find some lunch. I hitched into Gibraltar and found a splendid little Spanish restaurant where a rather boozy Major and I enjoyed a luncheon in the sun.

We arrived in Algiers later that day and the Transport Officer told me that there was quite a waiting list for flights to Italy. I told him that I was in no hurry and decided to take a few days unofficial leave. I was offered military accommodation but I thought I'd prefer the Alletti Hotel. I rediscovered Paul Lieven's Black Market restaurant and, of course, I paid my respects to the Sphinx.

Once we reached Italy I had to report to an IRTD (Infantry Reinforcement Training Depot) Camp near Caserta to the east of Naples. Like so many establishments of this kind it was run by a very pompous Lt-Colonel of a line regiment who had no doubt been promoted to Staff to get him away from his regiment. It was a common practice to promote unpopular officers or send them on continual courses to get them out of the way. In this case I could quite understand why no one would want such a petty little man cluttering up a good battalion. We took an instant dislike to each other and he soon revealed a deep loathing of the Brigade of Guards.

'What makes you think you're being posted to your Third Battalion? I might send you anywhere!'

I kept my temper with some difficulty and decided I'd have to find some way of getting up to the front on my own. The Gods were on my side. I had hitchhiked into Naples to look around when I spotted two Grenadier Officers in a Jeep. I flagged them down and discovered they were Lieutenant the Hon J. D. Berry and another subaltern from the Third Battalion. I told John Berry about the IRTD.

'We've had a lot of problems from that place. Jump in and we'll go and pick up your kit.'

'But . . .'

'Balls to the paperwork. We'll get the Adjutant to sort that out later. We're not going up for a couple of days. We're on a week's leave and we're staying in the flat.'

Apparently the Regiment had 'liberated' a flat at the top of the Via Roma from a grand Fascist. A wounded Guardsman who didn't want to go home was put in as caretaker and it was used by Officers on leave. It was, of course, quite illegal. It was a gorgeous flat and we made full use of it. That night we gave a party to some French Officers who were off to invade the South of France the following day. They had some very dishy French ambulance drivers with them who weren't sailing in the first batch. The following day we took some food and wine with us and drove the girls to Sorrento for a swim. By the time we got there we were smothered in volcanic ash because Vesuvius had recently erupted. It turned out to be a very romantic picnic.

The drive up to rejoin the Battalion gave me a chance, with John Berry's help, to catch up on the Third Battalion's progress up Italy. The 1st Guards Brigade had stayed in North Africa after the fall of Tunis until February, 1944. The Battalion landed in Naples on 5 February and were first in action in the salient on the Garigliano River followed by a battle on Monte Cerasola. The Battalion moved into the town of Cassino on 7 April and with the Coldstream on their right flank held it for 8 harrowing weeks. This was followed by a battle for Monte Grande south of Route Six near Arce where the Battalion suffered heavy casualties. After the fall of Arce the Battalion was engaged in the battle for Perugia. Captain Joshua Rowley, now commanding No 2 Company, who had been with me on the Montarnaud Farm patrol near Medjez, led the Allies into Perugia, to be greeted by cheering crowds of Italians and a warm welcome from the Mayor. In the battle leading up to the fall of Arezzo I was sorry to hear that Sergeant Lovett had been badly wounded, but I wasn't surprised to hear that he had been awarded the Military Medal. He was a very brave man and an excellent soldier.

The journey took two full days and we stopped overnight in a transit camp just outside Rome. The Germans had flooded the Pontine Marshes on their retreat and this had caused a plague of flies so dense that I wouldn't have believed it if I hadn't seen it. In the tented camp the Orderlies dropped mosquito nets over the entrance to the Officers' dining marquee before dinner and sprayed it with powerful insecticide. After about fifteen minutes they were able to sweep out a mound of dead flies about a foot high. Even then we had Italian POWs acting as waiters standing one between every two Officers to whisk the flies off each mouthful as we ate.

By the time we reached the Battalion late in July it had moved from Arezzo and was about to take up position on the east bank of the River Arno opposite the town of Monte-varchi. I was greeted with great warmth by the new CO, Lt-Colonel E. J. B. Nelson, who had commanded No 3 Company in Tunisia. He had replaced Colonel 'Johnnie' Goschen who had been my Company Commander at Sandhurst and who had in turn replaced Colonel Algy when he had been given a Brigade. In spite of the briefing by John Berry I wasn't really prepared for the changes there had been in the Battalion. After I had been wounded near Medjez the Battalion had been engaged in many actions, particularly the Battle of Djebel Mansour, where No 2 Company alone had fifty per cent casualties.

This was brought home to me when I went to visit my old No 4 Platoon in No 2 Company. I knew, of course, about Sergeant Lovett's wound and his MM, but I was saddened to find that there were very few of my old platoon left. There had been promotions of course, but the Platoon had suffered heavy casualties at Djebel Mansour and in later actions before the fall of Tunis. Two of the six survivors were West Country-men – Fortnum and Brooks – always known affectionately to us as 'Fortnum and Mason'. It was significant that they had been the oldest men in the platoon and Regulars before the War.

Colonel Nelson told me that I was to become 2nd in Command to Captain Tony Nation, No 4 Company. I was delighted because he and I had become good friends in No 2 Company when I had first joined the Battalion in Brigg. I was a little less delighted when Colonel John went on: 'No 4 is already in position in a villa overlooking Montevarchi. Tony is due for leave so I'm sending you up tomorrow to take over from him at once.'

I had hoped perhaps for a few days to settle in. On reflection I think I was very nervous at going back into action. It is a commonplace that young soldiers have the conviction that wounding and death is something that happens to other people. I certainly had that conviction until Medjez. It had gone.

As we approached the Battalion's forward positions the following evening at dusk there was a considerable amount of artillery activity on both sides. I must be honest and say that I was extremely nervous. My mouth was dry and my stomach and bowels became extremely noisy as we drove nearer to the action. I looked sternly ahead and hoped that my driver couldn't hear it over the gunfire.

Company HQ was in a villa on the forward slope of a hillside overlooking a very pretty valley with a village and medieval church perched on a hill the other side. The village was held by the Germans. The countryside was warm and gentle after the savage hills that the Battalion had been fighting in after Cassino and somehow war seemed quite out of place amongst the vines and peach groves.

CSM A. Dickinson greeted me and showed me into my Company Office which were also my living quarters and had a camp bed and blankets all neatly arranged. CSM Dickinson was a Brigade Warrant Officer of the very best sort who treated his Officers with respectful paternalism. It is often said that the Warrant Officers and NCOs run the Brigade and the Officers are just there for decoration. This is, of course, quite untrue. Some Guards Officers played up to this false image out of some misplaced sense of social vanity. Mercifully Officers of this kind were in the minority.

The CSM told me that Captain Nation was visiting the outlying platoons. One platoon was deployed round the HQ villa and the other two round farms and outbuildings on surrounding hillocks. We went outside just as the sun was going down and moving towards us through evening light was the bowed figure of a peasant wearing a large-brimmed straw hat and clutching a forked stick. I was astonished when the CSM saluted. I was even more astonished when the 'peasant' stepped into the shadows of the villa, straightened up and addressed me: 'Derek, how marvellous to see you!'

It was Tony Nation. He took off his absurd hat and handed it to me.

'You can have this. Comes in very handy when you're visiting the platoons. Less likely to be shot at!'

He gave me a short but efficient briefing. The Battalion's task at this time was to do no more than keep contact with the Germans – keeping them under constant surveillance by observation and patrols. We had to look for signs of their withdrawal which was expected to be imminent.

'Forgive me if I don't show you the positions. It's getting too dark and frankly I want to get off!'

I wasn't surprised. He looked very tired and drawn, as one would expect for an Officer who had been in almost continual action since the Battalion had landed at Naples in February. As he drove off in his jeep I realized how lucky I had been to have eighteen months out of the line.

I had just got my kit sorted out and asked the CSM to call me at dawn to visit the platoons and meet my Officers when a Captain in the Ayrshire Yeomanry walked into my room clutching two bottles of wine.

'David Veitch is the name. I have an OP upstairs and command my guns from here. How about a drink? It's local wine and not at all bad.'

He was marvellous company and our hilarious evening saw

off my nerves. It was hilarious because just as we were starting our second bottle we heard the most piercing female screams. We rushed outside to find a buxom peasant woman with a splendid black cavalry moustache being hotly pursued round the villa by an enormous Moorish deserter with his trousers over his shoulders and penis at the ready. It was all the Company Sergeant Major and three Guardsmen could do to restrain him, dress him and send him down the line under arrest. The woman was embarrassingly grateful. She opened her mouth in a broad grin to reveal decaying teeth that looked like a Colorado canyon and seemed to be offering David and me her favours voluntarily. We declined.

At first light the Company Sergeant-Major reported to me wearing an even more eccentric hat than the one Tony Nation had bequeathed to me. We did the rounds of all three platoons and I found that two of the platoon commanders had been my cadets. I fervently hoped that I had taught them properly. As I had expected the men were very well deployed and I knew I didn't have to make any changes.

During the short time that I had been going out on night patrols, night after night, in North Africa it had never occurred to me how anxious a Company Commander must be when he sends his subalterns out on dangerous missions. Now I was to find out at first hand. I had to send out probing patrols nightly and waiting for their return was often agonizing – particularly when there was gunfire heard from where I had sent them. I suppose I was lucky only to lose one Guardsman killed and five wounded over the three weeks before the Battalion was withdrawn for a rest.

Our relations with the Italian civilian population were very curious. Those Italians who followed Marshal Badoglio were technically our new Allies, while the rump of the Italian Army still loyal to Mussolini were our enemies. Fascists were often dragged up to Allied troops by Italian civilians and had to be screened through Intelligence. I had sent one such alleged Fascist back to Battalion only to be told that he had had to become a member of the Fascist Party when he became the local Station Master. He was, of course, released. A few days later he was dragged in front of me again. I took the initiative to release him myself. He was a mild-mannered little man with highly polished shoes and an immaculate suit. As I released him he almost cried and refused to leave – pointing to his wrist – his fingers – and his inside coat pocket. I asked Battalion HQ to send me an interpreter. Through him I learnt that the old man had had his wallet, his wedding-ring and watch taken by some Guardsmen in one of the outlying platoons. I sent for the Officer at the double.

'You will get this gentleman's possessions back here within the hour or you will be sent back under Close Arrest . . . and I expect you to bring the culprit back with you.'

He did just that. Looting of civilians by armed soldiers was something I just would not tolerate.

One night while David and I were lingering over supper during a welcome lull from German artillery activity a large group of heavily armed Italian civilians turned up outside the villa shouting excitedly.

'*Viva! Viva Inglese! Viva!*'

The last thing I wanted to do was attract further German shelling so I told the Sergeant-Major to get them inside under cover. Their leader, who described himself as '*Il Capitano*', shook me warmly by the hand and puffed garlic enthusiastically into my face as he declared: 'We Partigani! We fight! We fight for you – yes?'

Not quite knowing what the policy was about this, I did the weak thing and raised the Commanding Officer on the Field Telephone. John Nelson was not amused.

'For God's sake, Derek, don't bother me with them! Just send them off on a night patrol somewhere! I'll send you Rene Helling to interpret.'

Rene Helling was a young Luxembourger who had worn Grenadier uniform ever since the Battalion had 'borrowed' him from the Foreign Legion after the Battle of Djebel Mansour in Tunisia. He was an excellent linguist and a very brave man who would often go out on night patrols himself. His presence in the Battalion is a prime example of how the Guards bend the rules if it is to their advantage.

With Rene's help I showed *Il Capitano* two villages on the map. I told him that I wanted him to find out if the Germans, *Tedeschi* to the Italians, were still holding them. His eyes sparkled when I showed him the villages and he led his men off into the night with many *vivas*!

I reckoned it would take them no less than an hour and a half to reach both villages so David, Rene and I settled down to a bottle of wine.

After only half-an-hour there was an outburst of small arms fire in the valley and another half-an-hour later the Partiganis returned in a high state of excitement. The long-suffering Company Sergeant-Major quietened them down and led *Il Capitano* in to me. I pointed to one of the two villages on the map.

'Here . . . *niente Tedeschi* . . . *niente!*'

He pointed to the other village.

'Here . . . *multi Tedeschi* . . . *multi!*'

When I turned to Rene, he had a big smile on his face.

'What the devil is he up to, Rene? He can't possibly have had time to get to either village.'

'No! But you see he lives in the village where he says there are no Germans and his family have an ancient feud with the other village! He hopes very much that you will shell it!'

I gave up.

'Thank him very much and send him home. Tell him I will send for him next time I have a job for him – but for God's sake tell him not to come back here uninvited!'

After three weeks the Welsh Guards successfully moved forward through our position. The Battalion was then withdrawn to a tented Rest Camp on the banks of the Upper Arno. For the first time since I rejoined the Battalion I was able to see all my old friends in the Mess. There were sadly a lot of missing faces but it was rather like coming home. I knew all the Company Commanders – Captain David Rollo, MC, No

1 Company, Captain David Bonsor, MC, No 2 Company, Major John Jameson No 3 Company and I was temporarily commanding No 4 Company.

John Jameson had suffered a terrible double family loss on 18 June, 1944 when both his wife and mother were killed by the flying bomb that hit the Guards Chapel in London. He elected to stay with the Battalion which was a brave and sensible decision.

Joshua Rowley, who had been with me when I was wounded at Medjez, was still there and John Pearson-Gregory, the son of the Major Pearson-Gregory who had angrily 'killed' me on the TEWT at Windsor in 1940 when I had been idle after too good a luncheon.

The Regimental History has a lovely story about John after the successful battle for Perugia. During the post-battle confusion John and a few Guardsmen stumbled across a superior force of wandering Germans. A German Officer shouted: '*Hande Hoch! Schweinehund Englander!*'

John Pearson-Gregory looked down his nose at him with great disdain and said with full Grenadier authority: 'Come *here*, that German!'

'That German' meekly 'came here' and surrendered.

Evenings in the Officers' Mess marquee were very much enlivened by a full games set including a roulette wheel with ivory chips which had been 'liberated' from a German Officers' Mess. I had a spectacular run of luck and won a large amount of Allied Lire. This was money issued by the Allied military authority and was now the official currency in Allied-occupied Italy.

One night Joshua Rowley, John Pearson-Gregory and I were asked across to First Guards Brigade Mess to dinner. Dick Colvin, who had commanded our Battalion, was now the Brigadier and John Buchanan, who had been our Adjutant, was now his Brigade Major. It was a splendid evening of reunion. Over coffee the Brigadier gave us some news.

'By the way, I've just heard on the BBC that Florence has

been liberated. A beautiful city. If you haven't seen it I should take the opportunity before we go back into action. Mind you – you'll have to find a pretty convincing military reason for using the transport!'

He gave us a broad wink.

Our 'military' reason was that a partisan called Aldo, a former Savoy Grenadier Officer and a fervent Royalist, who had been invaluable to us both as an interpreter and a guide, had left us to return to his family in Florence. We told John Nelson, our Commanding Officer, who didn't believe a word of it, that we wanted to go in to Florence to persuade Aldo to stay with us for a bit.

The three of us set off in a jeep with a Guardsman driver and a good supply of Army rations. As we drove into Florence we were pleasantly surprised at how little damage had been done. The City looked so beautiful in the summer sunshine that we took our time before we tried to find Aldo's home. Aldo's address was 11 Via Magenta which was on the north side of the River Arno. All the bridges had been blown by the retreating Germans except the Ponte Vecchio which both the Germans and the Allies had agreed was not to be used for military traffic. That the beautiful Ponte Vecchio is still standing today is due to the fact that both sides respected this extraordinary agreement. A Bailey Bridge had been built by the Royal Engineers and was the only way to cross the river but to use it it was necessary to have a pass signed by the Provost Marshal. We went to see him and rather reluctantly he let us have one. We asked him what the military position was on the north side.

'Fairly stable. Germans have withdrawn to the foothills. A few Fascist snipers about, so don't loiter in squares or open spaces!'

Aldo's home, which he modestly described as a 'town' flat, was magnificent, with about nine bedrooms and beautifully furnished. Aldo appeared delighted to see us and introduced us to his very patrician family. They had a charming Argentinian couple staying with them The family were overwhelmed with the food we had brought and Aldo's father produced some excellent wine. It was a very civilized luncheon. The whole family and the Argentinians spoke perfect English and were prepared to celebrate the liberation of Florence from the Germans. It was clear that, like Aldo, the family were very anti-Mussolini and wanted the Royal Family reinstated as the rulers of their country.

When we had finished our meal Aldo suggested a tour of the city. We had sent our driver off with some money and orders to return in the late afternoon. We set off in the Jeep with Joshua driving and Aldo sitting next to him. Aldo turned to us in the back.

'John – I know your family own race horses back in England so I thought I would take you to the racecourse first then back into the city.'

I remember thinking it a bit surprising with the Uffizi Palace and all the other wonders of Florence waiting for us to explore and enjoy – but we'd had a good lunch so off we drove. There didn't seem to be anybody about as we drove rapidly across one square. I began to feel just a little uneasy. Why were there no British troops about?

We were driving up an avenue of trees with a park on our left and the racecourse on our right when it happened. One of the large trees had been felled across the avenue. A hatless soldier in tropical shorts and shirt was standing behind it pointing a weapon at us. Naturally we thought it must be one of our forward positions which we had been told was held in this sector by the Black Watch.

The young man was no Scot! He was a German. Joshua desperately tried to reverse – and stalled the jeep. John and I both tried to reach the Tommy gun in the back of the vehicle. Luckily we didn't because at that second two full sections of Germans rose from cover either side of the road with weapons at the aim. We had no choice but to raise our hands. We were prisoners.

VI

In the Bag

Aldo was led off first and we never saw him again. He was in civilian clothes and we were very worried that he might be shot. He wasn't and he survived the war.

At first we thought the Germans must be a patrol but as they led us back we saw slit trenches and we realized that we had blundered into a salient of the main German line. Our captors walked most cautiously along a taped track and ponted either side of it.

'*Achtung! Minen!*'

We believed them and made no attempt at a quick dash into the trees. We were taken to an outbuilding which was clearly a platoon HQ and I was bundled in front of a very young Lieutenant in parachutist uniform. He attempted to interrogate me. His English was studied but quite comprehensible.

'Where have you come from?'

'My name is Bond, my rank is Captain and my number is 138605.'

He studiously wrote this down.

'Now – you must tell me where you have come from and what is your unit?'

I decided to have some fun with him.

'Sorry – I don't understand you!' He repeated his question more slowly. I replied equally pedantically!

'SORRY-I-DO-NOT-UNDERSTAND-YOU!'

He blushed scarlet and lost confidence in his English. After taking Joshua and John's name, rank and number he decided

9. Playbill for *The Duke in Darkness*, Moosberg, November, 1944.

10. Jasper Grinling's portrait of the author, Moosberg, 1944.

to send us back for more expert interrogation. The amazing thing was that apart from checking us for side arms they did not search us at all. The first thing we were trained to do with prisoners was to take everything off them for examination which was why we never carried anything that could be helpful to the enemy into action. Of course we hadn't thought we were in action. We were on leave!

What was more amazing was that we were not searched when we reached what was obviously the Officers' Mess in part of the grandstand of the racecourse. The Mess was still at luncheon and, with the greatest courtesy, we were offered a glass of wine. I was the senior of the three of us and both Joshua and John looked at me.

'One glass only and no military questions!'

I needn't have worried. This was a Wehrmacht Parachutist Battalion and very 'Korrect' in their behaviour. It was clear almost immediately that they knew they had lost the war and the only thing they were worried about was making sure their families were safe from the Russians. They asked us which part of Germany would be occupied by the Western powers.

'We've no idea but anywhere west of Hamburg or Hanover should be OK.'

I was very conscious of the fact that in my pockets were letters from my wife addressed to me at Windsor with dated postmarks and a membership card to the Officers' Club in Naples – also dated. Clearly their Intelligence Officer would be able to deduce from the letters that I had been in England when the first flying bombs had landed. This would inevitably lead to lengthy questioning. I had to get rid of them. I asked to go to the latrine. An armed guard escorted me to an outdoor latrine and stood beside me with his machine pistol at the ready. I grimaced as I sat down and rubbed my stomach.

'Italian food! No good!'

He roared with laughter and went into some German lavatorial joke. As we were both laughing at it – although I hadn't understood a word – I used all my correspondence as lavatory paper.

We were to be taken back to some Divisional HQ for questioning and the vehicle they intended to use was an ambulance painted with the Red Cross. A Hauptmann with perfect English told us the reason.

'You will be safer from your English shells in it – but you must give me your parole not to escape.'

'As British Officers we are not allowed to do that. It is our duty to escape.'

'You would be very foolish to try. You might end up with the SS and they are *not* nice! You give me your parole?'

'Sorry!'

'Then I have to break Geneva Convention and send armed guards in an ambulance!'

We had two guards and a rather unpleasant Oberfeldwebel who was going back from the front to join a course. Both Joshua and John spoke German but we had been very careful not to reveal that to our captors. We soon discovered that neither the driver nor our guards spoke English so for the first time we were able to discuss escape. John had learnt from the driver that it was a good hour's drive to the HQ. We decided that at the first opportunity we would ask for a 'nature' stop and try for an escape then. We agreed that we would have more chance if we went off individually.

Very soon after we had left the front line area the ambulance was stopped at a road block manned by SS troops. They demanded to see the papers of all four Germans and scrutinized them in a very hostile manner. They then turned to us. Apparently they told the Oberfeldwebel that he was to hand us over to them. To do him justice the Oberfeldwebel flatly refused and showed his orders to take us to Divisional HQ. There was a hot argument but to our relief the Oberfeldwebel won and we drove on. The hostility between the Wehrmacht and the SS was very strong, resulting from the attempt on Hitler's life only a few weeks earlier. The SS thoroughly distrusted the Wehrmacht from the High Command down and were suspicious that they would attempt to make a separate peace. Hitler had given orders that the military salute was to be abolished and the Nazi salute was to be used at all times as a sign of loyalty to the Führer!

The ambulance stopped in a small town which had been badly shelled and bombed. It appeared that the Oberfeldwebel wanted to make a telephone call. We decided this was our opportunity. We pointed to our stomachs and by sign language asked if we could go to the latrine. Joshua stayed with the ambulance to split the two German guards. We had stopped outside a house which was a Signals HQ of some kind. There was no water supply so our guard led us through to the yard at the back.

'*Hier und schnell!*

I muttered to John, 'When I pull my pants up, off we go!'

Unfortunately nerves had taken over and I really needed to 'go'. John Pearson-Gregory was too quick for me and was over the end wall before I could get my shorts done up. The sentry saw him but before going after him bashed me on the head with his machine-pistol and pushed me, dazed, into the house. I thought in my dizzy way that if I walked through to the ambulance as if nothing had happened it might give John more time. Joshua had not had a chance as the Oberfeldwebel had returned soon after we had gone through to the yard.

As I came through there was a burst of firing from the back of the house. Germans appeared from everywhere. We were bundled into the back of the ambulance and locked in. After some little time and several bursts of machine-gun fire our guards opened up the ambulance. An SS Major stood glaring at us.

'Your silly friend is dead!'

His English was excellent.

'May I see the body and recover his personal possessions?'

'No, Herr Hauptmann, you may not!'

Joshua and I glanced at each other.

We both thought that the man was lying and John had made it. Our morale soared but not for long. We were taken from the ambulance by the SS and frog-marched to the local jail where we were thrown into a medieval cell with no windows, no light and no sanitation. Neither of us can really remember how long we were left there in total darkness. We carefully talked about 'shoes and ships and sealing-wax' and nothing military in case we were overheard. Nobody came near us with food or water and we were getting very demoralized in spite of singing to keep up our spirits. The lack of sanitation was particularly unpleasant and we began to stink.

We had no way of knowing how long we were in the cell before we were dragged out and taken in front of an immaculately-dressed SS Oberst and a mean-faced little civilian who was clearly Gestapo. The image we had always had of Gestapo was of big men with scarred faces in black leather overcoats. This little man was more typical. He was the sort of man you might be faced with in an Income Tax office if you had transgressed or were trying to get a permit for anything in any country anywhere in the world. The kind of little man whose bureaucratic powers make him feel big.

The Oberst looked at us as we stood there exhausted, unshaven and reeking of our own ordure.

'British Officers? These are British Officers?'

Then the questioning started. It was clear that they thought that there was some sinister purpose behind our driving straight into the German lines. I'm convinced they thought we were on some kind of mission to secure a surrender from the Wehrmacht – even on a local basis. The questioning was rough and unpleasant but it ended eventually – whether because they thought we were in fact idiots or because the Wehrmacht intervened we shall never know. The fact was that it was a Wehrmacht Officer who took us to be cleaned up and fed.

He and another Officer then drove us to the Divisional HQ, the one we had originally been bound for, in a small open car. I was sitting next to the Officer driving and Joshua was sitting behind with the other. I muttered to Joshua: 'The moment we stop anywhere we go for it!'

The Officer sitting next to me grinned and spoke in good English: 'I like London. I have been there often!'

He then tapped his revolver.

At the HQ we were given a more conventional interrogation and we reverted to the 'Name, Rank and Number' routine. They soon got bored with this and dismissed us. We were led out to the large marble entrance hall in the HQ villa where we were seated on a sofa beside a table covered with magazines. A Mess Corporal brought us sausage meat and bread with ersatz coffee. I didn't feel secure! I thought we might be 'bugged'.

'Cabbages and kings, Joshua!'

He nodded and we chatted away about gardening and the monarchy. One of the Officers who had questioned us, a rather charming Austrian Major, walked up to us with a map of Florence which he spread out on the table in front of us. He had a very pleasant manner and spoke perfect university English.

'Grub all right?'

'Thank you, yes.'

'By the way – just to save me a telephone call where exactly were you captured?'

I nearly fell for it and was just about to trace our route to the racecourse when I pulled myself up.

'Sorry – we're not here to save the Wehrmacht trouble.'

Angrily he snatched the map off the table and stalked off.

Shortly after that we were put into the back of an open truck with eleven other prisoners and driven off towards Bologna. As we drove through the foothills just to the north of Florence we saw hundreds of Italian prisoners and civilians digging big defences under the direction of armed German guards. We had been told in an Intelligence briefing that Kesselring was preparing a line of defence called the Gothen Stellung or the Gothic Line. This was why there had been very little resistance after Perugia and Arezzo had fallen and why there had been no attempt to defend Florence. The line was supposed to run from Pisa in the west to Rimini in the east.

From what we could see the defences were going to be very formidable and we knew that our Battalion would almost certainly be involved in breaching them. Speaking for myself I felt a deep sense of guilt that, through our stupidity, we wouldn't be taking part.

We were quite right in thinking the Battalion would be involved. On 17 September the 1st Guards Brigade forced a breach in the line in the Futa Pass and the Battalion captured Monte Pesciena which overlooked the Dicomano–Forli road. No 3 Company under the command of John Pearson-Gregory gained the peak after fierce hand-to-hand fighting. John had made his way back to the Battalion after his escape with the help of some Italian partisans.

Just to the south of Bologna we were taken to a medieval church by the side of the road and locked in. The church had been built right up against an escarpment of a hill in the Appena Tosco–Emiliano range.

Clearly this was a collecting point for prisoners. The priest's house at the far end of a passage between the church and the cliff was being used as a guardroom. A very unpleasant Sonderführer was in command. Sonderführers were a semi-commissioned rank somewhere between senior NCOs and Officers. The nearest equivalent in the British army would, I suppose, be Lieutenant and Quartermaster. However, they were certainly not Quartermasters and very often Sonderführers were Gestapo in uniform. This one certainly was.

Joshua and I were the only Officers in the church and there was one sergeant. The rest were other ranks from a variety of regiments. The Sergeant turned out to be something rather special. He had been captured behind the German lines working with Popski's Private Army, a very tough commando unit. After very heavy questioning his cover story, that he was a deserter, supported by faked letters from home about his wife's infidelity and an unposted letter from him to her saying that he was fed up and going to desert, had been accepted.

The three of us had a close look round the church to see if there was any chance of escape. We were allowed out into the passage for exercise and we pleaded to be allowed up to the front of the church to get into the sun. This gave us a good chance to look around. At first it looked hopeless but then we saw that the big double doors facing the roadway were hinged to swing inwards. We thought that if we could remove one set of hinges we could swing both doors open on the other. The windows of the church were very high and we couldn't see out without climbing up the curtains. One soldier shinned up to keep watch on the guard patrolling the passage while the rest of us hacked away at the wood round the hinges with any home-made tools we could find. Mine was a spoon which I sharpened on some granite in the wall.

Our lookout must have slipped for a moment because suddenly the side door burst open and the Sonderführer and three sentries with their guns at the ready charged in. They clubbed us into line with their rifle-butts and solemnly counted all fifteen of us.

The Sonderführer then strutted in front of me and glared at me.

'I haf a Spandau mounted outside those doors! If you or your men touch the doors again during the night I haf given orders for it to be fired! You will be moved on from here tomorrow!'

He then slapped me across the face with his gloved hand full force backwards and forwards several times.

'Typical English behaviour! Desecrating a church!'

Apparently to the Nazi mind using a church as a prison and putting latrine buckets behind the High Altar was not 'desecration'.

The following morning two sentries dragged me out of the church and into the priest's house. The priest was there in the corner of the room. He made the sign of the Cross over me and I feared the worst. I was wrong. The Sonderführer strode in.

'Sit down, Herr Hauptmann.'

As I sat I noticed there was a pot of ersatz coffee on the table and two cups. He poured the coffee and pushed a cup towards me.

'Last night I behaved incorrectly. Please forgive me.'

I was so taken aback that I mumbled: 'That's all right.'

'I know that it is your duty as a British Officer to escape. We Germans understand such things. Our countries should not be at war. We should both be fighting the Russians!'

I shrugged and sipped my coffee. He was silent for a moment, then he leant forward and shot a question at me.

'Why are you so friendly with that deserter? If you had been Germans he would have been hanged by now!'

I was very shaken because I felt I had placed the PPA Sergeant's life at risk by my own carelessness. I simulated intense indignation.

'In the British Army a man is innocent until he is proved guilty. When we have won the war – which won't be long – he will go on trial and if he is found guilty by a properly constituted Court Martial he will be punished!'

Mentally I kept my fingers crossed while he considered this. After a long pause he rose.

'Our Führer has now a Secret Weapon! He has told us so and *we* will win the war!'

Even this little Nazi did not speak with very much conviction.

'Later today many more prisoners will arrive and you will be driven to the north and then to Germany. You will soon see who is winning this war! I will keep the Spandau outside the church doors and any attempt to escape will be punished by death!'

When I got back into the church I told the Sergeant what had happened.

'Christ! I should have thought of that too, Sir!'

Later that morning two trucks drove up full of prisoners and we were herded into them. An armed guard sat with his back to the driving cab and another with his back to the tail board. An Obergefreiter sat next to the driver. All were armed with automatic weapons. As we moved off I threw a truly Guards salute to the Sonderführer who was startled into returning it with a military salute which he hastily converted into the Nazi salute.

Joshua and I managed to stay together but the PPA Sergeant was bundled into a different truck. I just prayed that he'd get through to a regular prison camp.

We were driven through Bologna and Modena and then northwards. As we approached the River Po we joined a very long queue of vehicles, most of them empty, waiting their turn to cross a pontoon bridge over the river. This was the German Army's main supply route and the pontoon bridge was vital. Whenever there was an Allied air-raid the bridge was broken and towed into either bank. We were within a hundred yards of the bridge when Allied planes came scream-ing over. All the Germans in the long line of vehicles dived for cover in the ditches but our guards stayed on our trucks with their guns at the aim. It was terrifying as the bombs rained down and débris whirled all round us. We felt like shouting: 'Steady on! We're on your side!'

Towards evening we reached Mantua. On the outskirts of the city there was a large transit camp. There was a central compound surrounding a small jailhouse which had cellars which were used as an air-raid shelter. We were housed in warehouse sheds all round it. Within the compound prisoners of all ranks and nationalities were allowed to intermingle. The whole camp had rather a temporary atmosphere because prisoners were only kept there until a full train-load was built up for transport to Germany. Outside the perimeter wire there appeared to be a swamp. Escape looked pretty hopeless.

There were several Officers among us but it turned out that I was the senior so I was sent for by the Kommandant. The Kommandantur was outside the wire through heavily guarded gates. The Kommandant himself was a Wehrmacht Oberst. He was Prussian and looked like a cartoon of a 'Hun' officer. However, he turned out to be a gentleman and a very decent man.

'Herr Hauptmann – as Senior British Officer I can give you this pass to come to see me at any time if you have complaints. You must give your parole not to use the pass for escape. Do you agree?'

I hesitated for a moment. He smiled at me.

'I know it is your duty to escape and I only ask your word that you will not use this pass for that purpose.'

'I give you my word, Sir.'

I took the pass and saluted him. He returned it with a smart military salute. That salute told me a great deal. Clearly the Kommandant was no Nazi!

The Officers had a shed to themselves and we were quite a mixture. There were British, Americans, French, Greeks and Italians – Badoglio Italians. An American Marine Major came to see me. He was particularly keen to escape as he had been taken prisoner once before and escaped – killing a German guard in the process. He was worried that the Germans would catch up with his records. He agreed to team up with Joshua and me. We began to examine all the possibilities.

In the meantime I had to take up my responsibilities as Senior British Officer. I called a meeting with some senior NCOs who had been in the camp for a few weeks and started to draw up a list of things to put before the Kommandant. Food came top of the list, of course, but there were several other things like the lack of proper washing facilities or hot water for shaving. I went to see the Kommandant.

'Sir, under the Geneva Convention prisoners of war are entitled to the same rations as their captors.'

'Really, Herr Hauptmann? Under which Section of the Geneva Convention is this said?'

I was stumped.

'I don't know, Sir. Perhaps we'd better look it up!'

He laughed.

'I do not have a copy, I fear. But I can save you the trouble because, believe it or not, your men *are* getting the same as my soldiers – who complain to me about it too. But you have your Red Cross parcels, don't you?'

'No, Sir.'

He looked surprised.

'I think you should see your Sergeant Smith in his Red Cross Store!'

I didn't even know there was a Red Cross Store. On my return to the compound I sought out an NCO.

'I want to see Sergeant Smith in the Red Cross Store. Where is it?'

'I'll take you to him, Sir. But he's a crook. You won't get anything out of him!'

'We'll see!'

One end of an other ranks' hut was screened off by a partition with a door which was locked. I knocked on the door and a very plump and surly sergeant peered out.

'Yes?'

'Yes, *Sir*! And stand to attention when you're talking to an Officer. And put that cigarette out!'

He gave me a very insolent look but did what I asked.

'Now – show me round the stores.'

For a moment I thought he was going to refuse, but I stepped forward and reluctantly he let me through. There were two equally sleek corporals inside who threw up sloppy and insolent salutes. The stores were full of battledresses and other Red Cross clothing and in one corner there was a stack of Red Cross parcels. On the table, incidentally, were the contents of several parcels – butter, jam, biscuits, Canadian dried milk called Klim and opened tins of bully beef and spam.

'Why haven't these parcels been distributed?'

'Not enough to go round, Sir. Besides we don't know when we're going to get any more.'

'You will make a distribution immediately – even if it is only one parcel between six prisoners!'

'But what's going to happen to us, Sir? You lot will get your parcels when you get to Germany. We've got to fucking stay here!'

'You, sergeant, are going to lose weight and if you continue to use language like that to an Officer I'll have you put in close arrest and see that you are stripped of your rank! Now you will distribute clothing first. Most of us are still wearing tropical kit. I'll call a Clothing Parade after Appell tomorrow morning. After the Parade there will be an issue of parcels, do you understand?'

'Supposing I refuse? I was officially put in charge of the Red Cross – Sir!'

'You will *not* refuse, sergeant!'

He didn't.

Appell was the morning roll call and although it was called by the Germans I asked the British contingent to treat it as their Commanding Officer's Parade and dress accordingly. I was supported in this by the NCOs who agreed with me that it was essential to keep up military discipline and morale. The count was made by German guards under the supervision of the Oberfeldwebel (Regimental Sergeant-Major). The Oberfeldwebel was a thoroughly unpleasant Nazi who spoke English with a Chicago accent. When the count was complete he marched up to the Kommandant to report and gave him a full Nazi salute. The Kommandant responded but always very subtly moved his arm from the Nazi salute to a military salute.

On the right of the Parade were two Badoglio Colonels who irritated me by hedging their bets and giving the Fascist salute. I decided to do something about it. I went to see the Kommandant.

'The Geneva Convention again, Herr Hauptmann?'

'No, Sir. A complaint about Appell.'

'Indeed?'

'Why are the Italians on the right of the parade?'

'I do not understand.'

'Well, Sir. We are your senior enemy – the Italians are your junior enemy. They should be on the left of parade!'

He chuckled.

'You are quite right, Herr Hauptmann. It will be corrected!'

It was. The following morning the crestfallen Italians were ignominiously dismissed to the left of the parade.

Joshua, the American Major and I had considered several escape ideas and dismissed them because they would take too long to set up and we knew that we had to escape before a full train-load was built up in the camp. We discovered that when the camp was evacuated the camp was virtually closed down for a week while the guards took leave. This formed the basis for our plan.

With the help of the Major's Marines who had been captured with him we prepared a hide under the bed-blocks in their hut and stocked it with food and water. The idea was that at the very last moment before we were marched to the train we would get into the hide and the Marines would make a 'phoney' hole in the perimeter wire. We hoped that the Germans would assume that we had escaped into the swamp, which incidentally was impossible, and we would lie up in the hide for 24 hours, or 48 if necessary, until the camp was empty and then simply walk out.

Looking back, of course, it seems like an idiotic plan, but then so many escape plans were and yet some of them came off. At least we were determined to try something before we arrived in Germany where the chances were reckoned to be very bleak.

I had to come to a decision about the large amount of Allied lire I still had on me – my ill-gotten gains from the roulette table. The first step was to change it into ordinary lire still being used in German-occupied Italy. I was told a Greek Officer could fix it. Greeks usually can. He discovered that one of the Fascist Italian Officers helping to guard us had family in Allied-occupied Italy and was anxious to get some money to them. The Greek struck a very good deal – and took a substantial commission.

It seemed unwise to put the money in the hide so I decided that I would try to get it through any strip search that might take place before we were entrained. That is, of course, if the hide idea didn't work. It didn't!

One day I was walking round the exercise yard with the Major when a British NCO rushed up to me.

'The train is in, Sir. They're shifting us today.'

We rushed back to our hut to get Joshua but he was finishing an exciting rubber of bridge.

'Join you in a minute!' I retired to the latrine where I rolled my thousands of lire into a hard stick and with the aid of a little German ersatz butter I pushed it up my bum. It was agony. I was only just in time. Suddenly the full complement of guards flooded into the compound. We were cut off from our hide.

I had thought that we would have been searched in our huts after we had collected our gear. I was wrong. They formed us up outside and counted us, then marched us off through the gates to the Kommandatur. As we marched along I felt my lire working loose, so by the time we reached the building where some of us were to be searched I was marching as if I had a bad case of piles. We weren't all told to strip but I had had a bad run in with the Oberfeldwebel and so I was one of those he picked out. I knew the roll of lire was poking out so I stood rigidly at attention to retain it. We had had the usual sauerkraut soup for lunch and I was afraid there might be a sudden involuntary distribution of largesse! Miraculously they didn't ask me to bend over and I got my bank roll through.

All the prisoners were loaded into cattle trucks – 60 prisoners to a truck and the doors secured fast from the outside. For the Officers it was even worse. We had 38 Officers in half a cattle truck. Barbed wire divided us from a squad of guards under an Obergefreiter. The wire ran diagonally across the truck with the doors on the guards' side permanently open. We had to take turns to sit down and our only sanitation was a sawdust box in the corner. We had saved a large empty German meat tin to pee into and empty out of the small slit windows. The conditions were appalling and we knew that as we were low priority traffic we would be on the train for days.

We tried to assess the possibilities of escape because we knew that once we were through the Brenner Tunnel and in Germany we would have had it. We noticed with some excitement that the barbed wire separating us from the open door on the guards' side of the truck was fastened to the woodwork on the inside of the truck. We decided to remove some of the barbs beyond the staples so that we could slip the single strands of wire through. We took turns at working away at it when the guards were resting or inattentive. We organized a little community singing to cover any noise we made. By the time we had reached Trento which took almost 24 hours we were very nearly there and we organized a draw for order of jumping. I drew 6.

We were stationary in a marshalling yard outside the city when the Obergefreiter got out of the train to collect rations for the guard. Unfortunately he walked under the truck window just as a prisoner emptied the meat tin full of pee. The Obergefreiter was drenched and was foolish enough to climb back into the truck with piss streaming down his uniform to yell at us. He got even more enraged at the hysterical laughter that greeted him and threatened us with his machine-pistol.

Before we moved off some Italian women who had been loading fruit on to a freight train came over to us and passed us fruit through the wire. When the Germans tried to stop them they yelled a stream of Italian invective at them. I only wish I had spoken Italian because whatever the women said totally unnerverd our guards who meekly allowed the women to pass us the fruit.

The journey then became very nerve-wracking. We had completed our work on the barbed wire and it was ready to pull open with a sharp tug. We had to choose a time when the train had slowed to a speed where we could jump without breaking our necks. Every time the train slowed the guards woke up and held their weapons at the ready. Several times we nearly started to jump without success. Eventually we reached Brenner Station on the Austrian border and pulled into a railway siding. The Obergefreiter told us that he would get us some coffee and bread. He went to swing himself out of the truck holding on to the barbed wire when the whole lot gave way and he fell flat on his back on the track! Of course we laughed – but not for long. The Obergefreiter and his guards went absolutely mad. I had always thought that it was the Latin races who were highly excitable, but Germans become very alarming when they lose control. They screamed at us: '*Hande hoch! Hande hoch!!*'

We all stood with our hands above our heads, not daring to move because they all had their fingers on the triggers of their machine-pistols. We must have stood there for at least half-an-hour while they counted us and re-counted us. The Obergefreiter then went away and returned with some staples and a large hammer. He handed them through the wire and pulled the wire back against the side of the cattle truck.

'Please to knock in!'

He came to the aim with his weapon so we complied.

We didn't travel very far that day and lay up in a siding until dawn. We then travelled through the suburbs of Munich in the early morning, stopping briefly at a suburban station. It was my bad luck to have my turn up by the wire because a group of ordinary middle-class German commuters gathered round the wire and spat at us. The hatred in their faces was frightening. Munich had been heavily bombed by the RAF at night and the Americans by day.

All the same I couldn't help wondering if the commuters at Surbiton would have behaved the same way to German prisoners. Who knows?

Our journey ended at a small Bavarian town called Moosberg. A large contingent of Germans were waiting in the goods yard where we were formed up in five ranks and marched into a large prison camp called Stalag VIIa. It had been built by French POWs in 1940 for 10,000 prisoners and had the standard arrangement of huts in separate compounds either side of the Lagerstrasse – the road running the length of the camp. All along the perimeter wire, which was about four feet thick, there were 'tiger' boxes at intervals, each manned by two guards with Spandau machine guns. It was a deeply depressing moment. All hope of escape seemed to have gone and we realized that we were likely to be imprisoned in this gloomy camp for the duration of the war.

Before being taken to the Officers' compound we were

made to line up before a very Prussian-looking Officer seated at a desk. He had a large ledger in front of him and he entered in each prisoner's name and number together with a POW number which he issued. By a remarkable coincidence my POW number was 138065 – almost the same as my British number 138605.

We were told to empty our pockets on to the table in front of him. I still had my soiled roll of lire. I had considered going through the agony of thrusting it up my arse again – but what was the use of lire in a German POW camp? As a gesture of defiance I handed it over. The Prussian looked at me with some surprise that I had got the money so far. He unrolled it and started counting it, moistening his fingers with his tongue between each note. I enjoyed every moment of it!

The moment we went into the British Officers' Compound we were besieged by the entire complement of 150 POWs wanting to know how things were going. How far up Italy had the Allies got? Was it true that the invasion of the South of France by the Americans and Free French had been swept back into the sea? Was it true that the flying bombs had laid waste to the whole of the south of England? I was able to reassure them on that point.

I had been in England when they started falling on London. I remember a day when John Stanley's brother Richard – also a Grenadier – and I were lunching at the Ivy when several flying bombs came over. The thing to do was to listen for the engine to cut out – then pray! It was uncanny in the restaurant as one bomb's engine cut out right overhead. The babble of conversation was silenced – forks full of food stopped short of the mouths – then after an agonizing thirty seconds there was a loud explosion nearby. Someone else had got it. Everything started up again as if a film director had shouted 'Action!'

Up until now Joshua and I – and indeed the other thirty-six Officers off the train – had not met any longer-term prisoners. We had only been captive for a matter of weeks and it came as something of a shock to arrive among Allied Officers who had accepted captivity as a fact of life. At this stage none of us off the train had accepted captivity. Most of the Officers in Moosburg had been prisoners for a year or more and some had been in Italian camps since 1941. Some had experienced a short period of freedom after Italy's surrender, and during the chaos that followed they lived with Italian families until they were rounded up again by the Germans. Some had tried very hard to rejoin the Allied lines. Some, it has to be said, had not.

The difference in attitude became very clear after we had been 'de-briefed' and it was our turn to ask questions.

'What about Red Cross Parcels?'

This was greeted with gales of ironic laughter.

'When – or perhaps I should say *if* we get any they are issued at the rate of one parcel to six POWs – so you had better form yourselves into syndicates of six. Makes it more civilized.'

'Escape?'

There was a moment's silence as the POWs glanced towards the Senior British Officer who was a Regular Major and, I regret to say, rather 'wet'.

'Unless you come up with a really good scheme don't waste the time of the Escape Committee. In any case at this stage of the war we don't want the Krauts unnecessarily upset!'

I could tell by the general reaction that some of my fellow prisoners were as contemptuous of this attitude as I was, so on our own initiative Joshua and I sought out the Escape Committee and discovered that there was a tunnel being dug from under the latrine hut. The latrine was a twenty-four-seater affair built over a deep septic sump the contents of which were sucked up from time to time into a tanker nick-named 'The Shit Machine'. The Shit Machine then drove out of the camp to a cabbage field in clear sight of our compound and emptied the sewage into troughs either side of rows of enormous cabbages. The cabbages were then used for sauerkraut soup which was fed to the POWs. It could be said to be perpetual motion in more ways than one!

We were told that we could, if we wished, volunteer to help dispose of the earth but that we would be right at the bottom of the escape list if there was a breakthrough.

The entrance to the tunnel was from under the last seat on the left in the latrine and it was strictly taboo for anyone to use it. One day a Greek Officer who believed in squatting on top of the seat in the Greek manner and who, through bad aiming, had earned the reputation of being a seat-crescenter, absent-mindedly arranged himself on the forbidden seat only to be impaled in the arse on a home-made entrenching tool wielded by a furious Welsh tunneller who caught him just in time!

Sadly for all the POWs who had been digging away for months the tunnel ended in disaster. One sunny day when the entire population of the compound was walking round and round the exercise area or playing football one of the large telegraph poles carrying the perimeter lighting slowly and gracefully sank into the ground. The tunnel had gone right underneath it.

The Germans went berserk. They rushed into the compound with guard dogs barking and yelping. Then we were lined up for an emergency Appell. Partly out of panic but mainly I suspect out of spite they kept us on Appell for at least two hours just when our lunch rations were due.

German rations at that time were:

Breakfast: ersatz coffee and 1 slice of coarse military bread.

Lunch: ½ bowl of soup and two or sometimes three potatoes boiled in their jackets – and mud.

Tea: Just tea! Also ersatz and quite undrinkable.

Supper: Two slices of coarse bread plus anything we had saved over from lunch.

The 'beverages' were delivered at the appropriate times in great buckets, but the solids were usually all delivered in one go at midday. Very occasionally we were given some suspiciously pink-red sausage – two slices per man. We noticed that this appeared soon after a raid on Munich. We called it Air-Raid Victim sausage.

139

We sat 14 to a long trestle table and the potatoes were delivered in 14-men ration buckets. It is difficult to believe now but food was of such overriding importance to us that we divided up into seven pairs and had a roster for sharing the potatoes out. Those at the top of the roster had the privilege of having the first choice of the carefully-laid-out rows of two-man rations – those at the bottom, i.e. the two laying the potatoes out, had the last choice. It was all taken very seriously, particularly when there were no Red Cross parcels. With some cunning, we managed to distribute our three pairs making up our syndicate through the roster to our best possible advantage.

We were a rather civilized syndicate. We had all been on the train together and had got on very well.

The four who joined Joshua and me were: Jasper Grinling, a Cavalry Officer, who was a Grinling of the Gilbey gin family and became Managing Director of the group some years after the war. He was a most accomplished artist and jazz musician and I've always been convinced that if he hadn't gone into the family business he would have made a name for himself in either field. I still have a watercolour portrait he did of me using red ink and sauerkraut soup, among other ingredients, to produce his colours.

Peter Langdon-Davies was studying for the Bar when he joined up and duly became a barrister after the war. His father was John Langdon-Davis, a distinguished science correspondent with a national newspaper. Peter had a great talent for languages, speaking German, French and Russian fluently.

Rupert Woolcombe was the quietest member of the syndicate – a charming man who was to become a country solicitor.

The sixth member was a Scot I shall simply call 'Jock' because I want to feel free to say some rather uncomplimentary things about him.

When Red Cross parcels arrived the six of us treated them as a communal larder and we took it in turns to be cook of the day. This gave us a little variety because each individual had different ideas of how to liven up the meagre German rations with the Red Cross food. Our cooking skills rather reflected our personal characters. Joshua was pretty slap-dash and inclined to burn things, Jasper and I were fairly creative if extravagant, Rupert was rather homely, Peter was excessively scientific in his approach and Jock was downright parsimonious. Although we cooked our food as a syndicate we usually ate it at the trestle tables with the others in our hut.

Our hut was very long and divided into three parts. There was a living area packed with triple-tiered bed-blocks, then a washhouse and a solid fuel stove which became the social focal point of the compound in the evenings. Then, the other side of the washroom, there was a second living area, half of which had been converted into a 'theatre'. Prisoners began to gather round the stove to cook their evening meals or merely to keep warm. The most popular supper dish was the remnants of the syndicates' potato ration mashed with a minute amount of bully beef or whatever else could be spared and packed into a greased soup bowl. This was then placed on top of the stove to brown, or when Joshua was cook, turn black. The stove area became the village green of the compound and the centre of political debate, story-telling and just plain 'line-shooting'.

As the weeks went by the new prisoners found themselves gradually being absorbed into the life-style of the camp and acquiring the camp language. We began to refer to ourselves as 'Kriegies' from the German for POW – Kriegesgefangener. The Germans, who were commonly referred to as Krauts in the Second World War, were more commonly called Goons in prison camp. Should a German wander into our compound there would be cry of 'Goon up!' as a warning to any Kriegies who were up to something illegal.

The camp had developed an internal economy of its own based on Red Cross parcels and cigarettes. There were four different kinds of Red Cross parcel – British, American, Canadian and occasionally Argentinian bulk parcels which were very popular. The food varied and on balance the Canadian were the best parcels, containing, as they did, a pound tin of butter, Spam, pressed beef, biscuits, Nescafé and Klim. Klim – milk spelled backwards – was excellent dried milk. On very special occasions – like birthdays – we would have a Klim-bash which was Klim made into the consistency of cream loaded with jam on to Canadian biscuits which had been soaked in water and miraculously turned into waffles in a frying pan. Forty-five years later my mouth still waters at the thought.

All parcels contained cigarettes and they became the currency of the camp. German-speaking Kriegies would bargain with the German guards for black market food. When we arrived the going rate for a German 'civilian' loaf of bread was ten cigarettes. Later an influx of American prisoners caused inflation and it rose to fifteen cigarettes. The loaves were smuggled in by the guards in their gas-mask cases or, less palatably, taped to the insides of their thighs.

The Germans had allowed individual parcels from prisoners' families earlier in the war and those who had been unlucky enough to have been prisoners that long at least had the compensation of becoming the capitalists of the compound with their reserves of cigarettes. They were the rich Kriegies.

Others created their own wealth with their manual skills. They made kitchen utensils out of old Red Cross tins – saucepans, billy-cans, frying-pans and 'stoofahs', which were personal cookers known as Smokeless Cookers or Cookless Smokers according to the skill of the individual cook! A stoofah consisted of a cooking plate over a combustion chamber into which was fed scraps of combustible material of all kinds. Connected to the combustion chamber was a Klim tin containing a revolving fan made of pieces of tin on a spindle connected to a spool on the outside of the tin which was in turn connected to a spool on the outside of the tin which was in turn connected to a fan belt made of string to a bigger wheel with a handle. The faster you turned the handle the fiercer the flame became but the faster you burnt your fuel. Most of the fuel was provided by shaving pieces off the inside of the hut in such a way that the Goons wouldn't detect it. Towards the end of the war many huts were matchbox thin! All these excellent pieces of kitchen equipment had their price in cigarettes and the skilled makers would hammer away all day and become fairly well-off.

Because the contents of the Red Cross parcels varied so much the prices of the various items changed according to the rumours of whether there were American, British or Canadian parcels on their way from Munich – or indeed whether any parcels were on their way at all. Two enterprising prisoners spotted the commercial possibilities of this situation and set up a Commodities Market. They didn't call it that – but that's what it was. They acquired a stock of Red Cross food with cigarette capital raised for them by 'investors', then marked up their prices daily. Rumours of the imminent arrival of British parcels for instance would send the price of porridge plummeting! They became very rich – but they also provided a service.

I suppose that it was inevitable that in such a thriving capitalist society Socialism should rear its ugly head and, sure enough, a group of Officers approached the Senior British Officer with the argument that as we were all on the edge of starvation any food coming into the compound should be shared out equally between us all. The more extreme of them even thought that those capable of making kitchen equipment should hand it out free to all and sundry out of pure love of mankind! A capital tax was even proposed to punish the rich and prudent Kriegies and distribute their cigarette wealth amongst us all. The SBO firmly rejected the last suggestion as he and a group of other Majors were very wealthy and lived a comparatively sybaritic life in their cosy little enclave at the warmest end of the hut. They were known to the rest of us as the Fujima Boys – Fuck U Jack I'm Alright! As a concession the SBO did permit the 'nationalization' of black market food coming into the camp as an experiment. The immediate effect was that the German-speaking Officers withdrew their services and the black market dried up. After a week the compound happily re-embraced capitalism However, the political debate continued round the stove in the evening for weeks.

There was another group of Officers who found it difficult to repress their natural Christian charity towards the poor, but as we were all equally paupers in the camp they had to look outside our compound. They didn't have to look far. Russian Officers were in the next compound to ours and were treated appallingly by the Germans. Furthermore, the Soviets did not subscribe to the Red Cross or any equivalent charitable organization and therefore they had no parcels. Nor did they have any hope as, at the time of Stalingrad, Stalin had issued the order that any Russian Officer allowing himself to be taken prisoner would be executed on his release. Collections were organized whenever Red Cross parcels were issued and I am proud to say that every syndicate contributed generously, although we had so little to spare. As a Russian-speaking Officer, Peter Langdon-Davies must take a lot of credit for this.

One of the rich Kriegies was Captain Eddie Bruen who had been attached to the Indian Army. He was very regimental. He very much admired my Herbert Johnson Service Dress cap which I had been wearing when I was taken prisoner. After all I had been on leave. He kept trying to buy it off me and at first I refused him out of regimental pride. It was, after all, a Grenadier cap! However, he was determined to acquire it.

'Tell you what, Derek, I'll give you *ten* civilian loaves over four weeks starting now! How about it?'

The others in my syndicate didn't say a word. They merely gazed at my hat longingly. They were mentally slicing it into mouth-watering slices of fresh civilian bread. I gave in. Over the next week or two we ate my hat!

With the chances of escape now so remote, we increasingly joined the longer-term prisoners in turning our minds in from the wire and taking part in the miniature society within the compound.

Everyone pursued their personal leisure interests. There were bridge and chess tournaments. Those with specialist knowledge gave lectures and courses. There was a very hot poker school and I had such a bad run that I had to give up smoking to pay off my debts.

At this stage of our imprisonment we still had space for a small theatre at one end of our hut and I decided to put on a play. The Red Cross and other organizations at home had sent over a number of plays for this purpose. Unfortunately most of them were farces and amateurs are always notoriously bad at farce. Other forms of drama suit them better because their sincerity and enthusiasm can cover a multitude of sins. About the only one that seemed suitable was Patrick Hamilton's *Duke in Darkness*. This appealed very much to me as it had an all-male cast and furthermore the theme of the play was escape. I thought this might appeal to POWs.

In theory prisoners of war could ask their captors for help in their cultural activities. We had one third of our pay deducted at home which was supposed to be available to us in prison camp for this purpose. The play was set in medieval France and we would therefore need costumes as well as a few props. I applied to see the Sonderführer who was supposed to be in charge of Welfare. Like most Sonderführers he was really Gestapo, so I wasn't expecting much.

'Sit, Herr Hauptmann, sit! Now what can I do for you?'

'We want to put on a production of this play. You will see from this copy that it has been passed by your censors.'

'Censors? We Germans never censor the arts! This stamp here merely means it is suitable!'

I restrained myself with some difficulty.

'*The Duke in Darkness* – Ja! I am sure I have heard of it!'

I was quite sure that he hadn't.

'As you will see it is a period play and we need costumes and props.'

'Props? Ah yes, *props*! Like you use for your tunnels, ja?'

'No – of course not. Props is short for Properties. Things needed in the play – like swords, ropes, candles, goblets. Of course we'd give our parole that they would not be used for escape.'

'I see – I see! Well I had better make a list of these Props – ja?'

Perhaps I had misjudged him. I handed him the lists of costumes and props and started to read out the props list in case he objected to any of them.

'Ten large candles.'

'Ja.'

'Preferably red.'

'Ja! Ja!'

'A rope – twelve feet long.'

'Feet? What is "feet"? How long in metres?'

'Er – I'll let you know.'

We worked our way through the list with the Sonderführer painstakingly writing it all down. When I had finished he looked up at me.

'Nothing else, Herr Hauptmann?'

Although I was senior to him I thought his co-operation was worthy of a 'Sir'.

'No, Sir, and I'm most grateful!'

He looked at me for a moment without speaking. Then a sadistic smirk came over his face.

'You can't have any of it, Herr Hauptmann, *nothing*!'

I drew myself up to attention, did a Guards' about-turn and marched out without saluting. He called out after me but I ignored him. I wasn't going to plead with the little bastard.

I now approached the practically unemployed Escape Committee and asked for their help.

'Leave it to us, Derek. We'll work something out. You just get on with your rehearsals.'

Calling rehearsals became extremely difficult. One would not have thought that availability would be any kind of problem. How wrong I was.

'Sorry, Derek, can't make 10.30 . . . my French Course . . .'

'Sorry, old mate, Chess Tournament Finals!'

or

'For Heaven's sake! Where's John?'

'Turned his face to the wall!'

146

'Turning one's face to the wall' was a POW euphemism for having a nervous breakdown. We didn't realize that at the time, of course. Suddenly a prisoner would retire to his bunk and not talk to anyone for maybe two or three days. We discovered that the best policy was to let them work it out for themselves. All we tried to do was to get them to eat. One day the prisoner would resume 'normal' camp life as if nothing had happened and nobody commented on it.

When the set was nearly ready I went to the electrician who had done the lighting for the tunnel with a request.

'How can I set about getting a "Dim-out" on the back-cloth?'

'My dear fellow – no problem. I'll make a water resistance!'

I have always been hopeless at anything electrical or, for that matter, anything where I am required to use my hands skilfully.

'Splendid – go ahead!'

One evening we decided to try it out during a lighting rehearsal. With supreme confidence our electrician operated his 'water-resistance'.

It fused all the lights in the block! The sirens went and the guards came racing in with their guns and guard dogs, clearly convinced that an escape plot was afoot. Once they had calmed down and gone through the routine counting process they traced the electrical fault to our little stage. They decided to punish us by smashing up the whole set including the footlights and spots made so painstakingly out of Klim tins.

For a moment we watched them in despair – then we joined in and helped.

'Want this smashed? Right!' Crunch!

As we threw ourselves with enthusiasm into the orgy of destruction the Germans stopped and stared at us. Then, puzzled and defeated, they moved out. We had all the time in the world to rebuild the whole thing.

I still got my Dim-out. An ingenious prisoner stuck amber

cellophane from the Argentinian parcels on to frames of cardboard which were lowered frame by frame on threads of cotton over the lights. It was most effective.

The play was a reasonable success within its limitations. However, it was rather a depressing play in our situation. For instance the Duke, played rather lugubriously by the Senior British Officer, had lines to his faithful Voulain like: 'The fifteenth summer – followed by the fifteenth autumn – followed by the fifteenth winter . . .'

In the fortnightly revue following the play some wags presented a hilarious sketch, wearing our costumes which had all been made out of Red Cross clothing. Its title – 'Fifteen Years Without a Red Cross Parcel!'

The fortnightly revues alternated every other Saturday with 'In Camp Tonight', a chat show in a mock-up BBC studio. POW 'Personalities' were interviewed in front of a mock-up microphone and they indulged in outrageous 'line-shoots'. My favourite was by a Maori Officer, inevitably nicknamed Kiwi who, incidentally, ran the Red Cross. He described how he was wounded at Alamein and the climax was when he bared his stomach to show five bullet holes in a neat circle round his navel. His stomach muscles had been so strong that very little damage had been done to his intestine.

The fortnightly revues were a little more elaborate. Most of the sketches were reconstructed from revues one or other of us had seen in London, but we had some very good original material written by Kriegies. Jasper Grinling was an expert jazz pianist and managed to get a very good trio together with a clarinettist and a violinist who, I'm afraid, was no Stephane Grappelli.

To our intense annoyance the Kommandant began to invite himself and his Staff to our revues and insisted on seats being reserved in the front row. A regular sketch contributor came to me with an idea.

'We want to do the Kommandant and his gang arriving in our theatre.'

'Not a very good idea! They'd close down the bloody thing.'

'You don't understand. We get the audience in *before* the Kommandant is due to arrive and then do the sketch before curtain up!'

Frankly I thought it rather a feeble idea but I was out-voted and it was arranged.

On that Saturday night the audience rather resented being hustled into the recreation area half-an-hour ahead of the advertised time and were therefore 'sitting on their hands'. Four POWs dressed fairly convincingly as the Kommandant and his Staff entered from the rear and approached the reserved seats. As they moved towards their seats they suddenly started to react towards the audience – at first with bewilderment and then with mounting anger. There was mild laughter and desultory applause. I thought that I had been right all along about the sketch.

Then the real Kommandant and his Staff strutted in. The whole audience began to laugh. The Kommandant looked bewildered and checked his fly-buttons. The laughter became hysterical. His bewilderment turned to anger. By this time we were literally crying with laughter. His Staff started to gesture and shout at us. The laughter was uncontrollable. The POWs in the sketch had anticipated every minute reaction with devastating accuracy. How long it would have gone on I don't know, but the Senior British Officer leapt to his feet.

'Gentlemen! That is enough!'

Once the audience had finally settled down the curtain went up on the concert – but it was a very difficult act to follow. The Kommandant never came again.

Debate amongst us was by no means confined to politics. Many of the Officers had very good academic backgrounds and raised the level of philosophical and religious debate to very high levels indeed. Having missed out on a university career, I found this very stimulating and enriching. These debates were mostly informal and took place huddled round the stove after our evening meal when we had tired of the usual tedious round of bawdy Rugby choruses.

However hard we tried to escape from the realities of our

149

situation by creating our own little world, one question hung over us all the time. How long?

We had occasional bulletins from a secret radio which was only assembled sparingly from time to time for security reasons. Otherwise we relied on the newly-arrived prisoners to bring us up to date with the war and combat the highly corrosive effect of German propaganda. For instance the arrival of the prisoners taken after the Arnhem disaster confirmed rather devastatingly what the Germans had been telling us about it and thereby gave credence to other claims of theirs which were totally false. Morale was very low at moments like this.

One thing the German propaganda did achieve was a unity of purpose among us to make life as difficult as possible for our captors. Although our tunnel had collapsed and escape plans had dwindled to a few hair-brained schemes promoted by the eccentric, we saw no reason not to make the Germans think mass escape or even individual escape was imminent.

One of the funniest of these 'phoney' escape attempts followed the rumours that had infiltrated into our camp of the Wooden Horse escape. The Germans were highly suspicious of any sporting equipment after the Wooden Horse success. We made a see-saw and, to the astonishment of the guards, grown men would see-saw up and down for hours. Day by day the see-saw was eased nearer to the perimeter wire until one end was nearly over the Warning Wire. The Warning Wire was a single strand of wire about ten feet from the main wire mounted by a notice which read: WHEN ONE CROSSES THE WIRE THERE WILL BE SHOOTING!

The see-saw was left out until dusk and then, with overt furtiveness, a tiny Officer was rushed out of the hut and placed on one end and three hulking great Officers made as if to leap on the other and catapult him over the wire. The guards in the tiger box took it absolutely seriously and sounded the alarm!

The morning Appell was considered by the British prisoners to be their own Commanding Officer's Parade. The fact that the Germans counted us and then reported us present and correct to the Kommandant was incidental. Obviously the reason for this was one of morale. We all turned out properly, if rather shabbily, dressed and shaved. We maintained our standards of drill when coming to attention and when we received the command from the SBO 'Parade Dismiss!'

Some of our Allies, particularly the Americans, totally misunderstood this and considered us to be toadying to the Germans. Nothing could have been further from the truth. We kept our own self-respect and the respect of our enemy. Those who turned out unshaven, scruffy and with their hands in their pockets did not. They looked like a defeated army. We did not.

Any other Appell − called for whatever reason − was another matter and we did our best to make them as awkward and difficult for the Germans as possible. There was one very unpleasant SS officer who had the infuriating habit when he was on night duty of calling an Appell in our hut in the small hours of the morning. We decided to teach him a lesson. With careful rehearsal we worked out a drill so that at each count he had a different number of prisoners.

It was quite simple really. We had to stand in five ranks between the two rows of bed-blocks. As soon as the Leutnant and his Unteroffizier had counted past a particular point two or three prisoners from the top of the count would duck under the bed-blocks and join in at the other end. We rehearsed it so that every count was different but always with too many prisoners. Then we changed the drill and caused there to be two missing.

That was when the fur really began to fly. Dogs were brought in and then we would risk just one more count of too many prisoners before standing correctly for a final count. Of course when it was correct the Leutnant just wouldn't believe it.

In carrying out these little exercises we had to judge the Germans' volatile nature with some care. When the dogs were introduced it was a sign that we had pushed them to the limit.

The dogs were not always as frightening as they seemed, although one Free French Officer was dragged back into the compound after he had tried to escape from a Parole Walk. He had terrible bites all over his body. The Germans brought him in to our hut so that we could see the state he was in before he was taken off to have his wounds dressed.

On the other hand we saw the most extraordinary incident take place in the NCOs' compound which was next to ours on the other side from the Russian Officers. It was during an air-raid. As soon as the air-raid siren sounded all prisoners were supposed to return to their huts immediately. On this particular day a sergeant was just bringing water for his tea to the boil on his stoofah when the siren went. Nothing was going to move him. He quietly ignored the guards' shouts of 'Raus! Raus!' and stubbornly went on feeding in the fuel and cranking the handle. The guards didn't like it! They released a dog towards him. It charged across the compound with fangs bared and barking hysterically.

We watched in horror as it reached the sergeant. The dog stopped. Its barking turned to a friendly whine and it fawned against him and licked his face. The Germans went mad. Two guards rushed over, kicked the sergeant, kicked the dog harder, smashed the stoofah and dragged the sergeant away – still kicking the dog in a frenzy of rage.

The following day a notice went up in all huts:

IT HAS COME TO THE NOTICE THAT
GUARD DOGS OF THE RED CROSS PARCELS
HAVE BEEN FED!
THIS PRACTICE WILL CEASE!!
THE DOGS WILL NOT ACCEPT THESE RATIONS!!!

In November, 1944, we suddenly got an issue of Red Cross parcels, six to a parcel, three weeks running. The pessimists put a little aside for Christmas but our syndicate believed in living for the moment. God knows what the future had in store for us. The one who didn't agree was Jock.

11. *The Captive Heart*, 1945.
Left to right: Guy Middleton,
Jack Lambert, the author, Basil Radford.

12. Moosberg, Spring, 1945 – the syndicate:
Captain Joshua Rowley, Captain Jasper Grinling, Captain Peter Langdon-Davies,
Captain Rupert Woolcombe, Captain Derek Bond.

13. 29 April, 1975 – re-union of the syndicate.

'I don't want to be in a syndicate any more. I want my sixth of the parcels on my own.'

We couldn't dissuade him and he would give us no reason. If he wanted to be a loner it was up to him. It made it damned awkward. How do you divide a tin of condensed milk into six? We had all got on very well with rations up to this point – except, that is, for the condensed milk! The condensed milk had caused considerable friction. I thought it better to use it undiluted because it seemed sweeter that way. Peter Langdon-Davies wanted it diluted and said that it was scientific nonsense to say the milk 'seemed' sweeter when still condensed.

'. . . and I ought to know because my father is Scientific Editor of the *Daily Mail*!'

'I don't care if your father is Professor Einstein – I know my own taste buds!'

Apparently this was an on-going and serious argument between us that drove Joshua and the others mad. We have often laughed about it after the war – but little things seemed to matter such a lot in the camp.

What certainly did matter was theft. One day a Kriegie reported that food had been taken from his pack. At first this was discounted as part of the paranoid obsession that hungry Kriegies always had about food. However, a watch was kept and unhappily an Officer was caught in the act of stealing food. He was reported to the Senior British Officer.

It was an appalling dilemma. How do you deal with a thief in prison camp? Hand him over to the Germans for punishment? Out of the question. Administer corporal punishment? Which Officer is going to hold him down and which is going to wield the stick? Cut off his Red Cross Parcels when we were only a tiny margin above the starvation line?

The SBO discarded all these options and made a disastrous decision. He set up a formal Court of Enquiry to assemble evidence for a possible Court Martial back in England after liberation.

Nothing could have been crueller. It stripped the poor wretched man of the one thing that kept us all alive and sane

– our thoughts of home and family. Not only that. He had no way of expiating his crime and being accepted back into 'normal' camp society. Inevitably he 'turned his face to the wall' with a vengeance.

Several of us signed a petition on his behalf and took it to the SBO. The SBO was a Regular Officer who had been forced to surrender his command to the Germans but brooded on the circumstances under which he did so. No doubt this affected his thinking. It could be that, as a Regular, he felt he had to play it by the book to put his record straight when we got home. Who knows? For whatever reason he would not budge from his decision to hand over the record of the Court of Enquiry to the British Army on repatriation.

Nobody could help the accused man, although the Officer who had reported him, to do him justice, fussed over him like an old hen when the poor man 'turned his face to the wall'. Perhaps the accuser felt a little remorse.

I believe the Court of Enquiry was simply torn up by the authorities on liberation but the damage had been done and the wretched man never returned to normality. I have not heard what happened to him afterwards on repatriation.

The whole business affected me deeply and some time after the war I wrote a play based on the story for BBC Radio Four called *Sentence Deferred*.

Parole walks were still permitted at that time but one of the final ones in November ended in a nightmare. One thing we particularly lacked in our diet was Vitamin C and, although tablets were included in the American parcels, the deficiency was so bad at times that if a prisoner barked his shin on a bench the graze would not heal but ulcerated. For this reason prisoners on the walks would take chocolate, tea, real coffee and other things from the Red Cross parcels which were in short supply in Germany to exchange for fresh vegetables with local farmers.

On this particular walk the POW column encountered a column of political prisoners being marched to Dachau by the SS.

They were wearing the striped pyjamas that are now so hauntingly familiar to us from horror documentaries and they were so gaunt and dehumanized that the exercise of marching them anywhere seemed superfluous. Most of them were clearly dying.

One or two Kriegies offered the poor creatures anything edible they carried. To the horror of the POWs, the political prisoners snatched the food like wild animals and fought each other over it, tearing at each other with claw-like hands. The SS guards then brutally clubbed them back into line and started to club the POWs. The Stalag guards were mainly Volkssturm – the equivalent of our Home Guard – and tried to protect the POWs from the SS. It turned into a nightmarish four-way scuffle which was only broken up by a passing Wehrmacht Major. The POWs returned to camp thoroughly shaken. They had seen for themselves that the horror stories of the concentration camps were true.

Our syndicate recruited a Polish Officer to make up our six-to-a-parcel in place of Jock who we sent off to fuss over his own arrangements with his Red Cross rations. His name was Lew Kurylowitz and he had been a fighter pilot in the Polish Army Air Force. He had been shot down over Eastern Poland in 1939 by the Russians and taken prisoner by them. Many of his brother Officers were executed – merely because they were Officers. He was lucky – if you can call being starved and beaten for months on end lucky. When Hitler attacked his erstwhile allies, the Russians, Anthony Eden, then British Foreign Secretary, did a deal with Stalin and all Polish POWs in Russian hands were permitted, if they wished, to join the Free Polish Army in Britain. Lew came to Britain and flew with the RAF – only to be shot down and taken prisoner by the Germans.

All Poles taken prisoner by the Germans while fighting with the British were deemed to be British mercenaries and were therefore treated to all intents and purposes as British. This was just as well for Lew because the Poles in our camp who had been captured in 1939 were treated appallingly and many died as a result of the atrocities they suffered.

Lew made it his business to list these war crimes for evidence against the perpetrators after the war. He had been badly wounded when shot down and still had a piece of shrapnel lodged at the base of his skull. This meant that he frequently had to attend the German hospital for treatment. The hospital was the one place where all ranks and nationalities were allowed to mix. It was odd that the Germans, or at least the Wehrmacht, respected the Red Cross under which the hospital was conducted. During his visits Lew compiled a comprehensive list of murdered Poles and the SS officers who were responsible. It was a very courageous thing to do. Had he been caught, at the very least he would have been sent to a concentration camp.

Lew, with every good reason, was very concerned about the fate of Poland after the war. He drew us a map of his country and the borders with Russia as they existed in 1939. He asked us how the map would look when we won the war. It was a deeply embarrassing question.

We mumbled vaguely about 'the Curzon Line' and indicated on his map roughly a line north and south through Brest-Litovsk.

'So!' he said. 'You come into the war because you guarantee the Polish boundaries, is that not so?'

'Er . . . yes.'

He pointed on his map to the Polish Corridor and Danzig.

'So we Poles and you our British allies go to war over this little piece. We win the war and we lose this great big piece?'

There was no answer to that.

For some reason the Germans suddenly decided that although Lew was a Polish Army Captain he was a pilot and therefore technically in the RAF and should be sent to Stalag Luft 3.

This caused Lew considerable anxiety about his lists as he knew he was bound to be searched thoroughly on leaving the camp. He asked me to keep them and hand them over to the Allies when we were liberated. I must confess I was rather worried about it, but it was the least I could do. I crinkled the sheets of paper as much as I could without making them illegible and inserted them into the lining of my battledress.

A week or two after Lew had gone I suffered from a bad duodenal ulcer and was admitted to hospital for a short time where there were Red Cross invalid parcels. It was something of a treat as they contained creamed rice and other bland foods and I was eating an almost normal amount of food for the first time since capture. In the next bed to mine there was a young Russian Officer who spoke excellent English. He was full of questions about the standard of living in England but wouldn't believe what I told him.

'I understand you have to tell me these things because you are a British Officer – but I have read my Dickens! Don't worry – when we have beaten the Germans we will come and liberate you from capitalism!'

One day the Gestapo swooped on the camp for a surprise search. This happened every now and again. Without warning – even to the Kommandant – a convoy of cars would drive into the camp and Gestapo Officers, some in uniform and some in plain clothes, would search even the German guards at random. Any German possessing Red Cross parcel materials would automatically be shipped off to the Russian Front.

Two thoroughly unpleasant Gestapo men in plain clothes stamped into the ward of the hospital and started to search everybody and everything in sight – even making very sick prisoners climb out of their beds.

My battledress jacket with Lew's list in the lining was on the chair by my bed. When it came to my turn I thought I was going to be lucky because the man searching me didn't appear to notice the jacket. To my horror his colleague did. He picked it up and ran his hands down the lining. I tried not to look. I just prayed.

At the very moment that the Gestapo man was feeling along the lining of my battledress a German male nurse turned to leave the room with a bedpan. The Gestapo man dropped my jacket and grabbed the nurse by his arm to search him. I was safe.

Two days after we were liberated, Officers from the War Crimes Commission visited the camp and I was able to hand the lists over.

One of my most moving memories as a POW is of the arrival of the survivors of the Warsaw uprising towards the end of the war.

After Hitler and Stalin had joined forces to crush Poland in 1939 a Polish Resistance was formed in the débris of what had been Warsaw. Old men, sick men who had been unfit for military service, youths and schoolboys drilled in secret under the Nazi occupation and waited for a signal from the Allies to rise up and take their city back. They even managed to dress themselves in home-made uniforms.

After the Russians had driven into Poland and captured Lublin on 23 July, 1944, a Polish Committee of National Liberation was formed. It was, of course, a Communist-dominated body committed to establishing a Soviet-dominated Republic of Poland. These Polish Communists broadcast from Moscow on 29 July, calling on the Polish Resistance to rise up against the Germans and on 1 August the secretly trained army went into action.

The Russians cynically turned the advance of their main armies south, leaving the Polish Resistance to fend for itself. After all, the Russians thought, they were only bourgeois and middle class with no place in the glorious new Polish Soviet! The Western Allies tried desperately to persuade the Russians to allow them to use air bases for relieving planes to land and refuel. The Russians cruelly refused. The Resistance fought the Germans with enormous courage until 2 October when the revolt succumbed to the superior German forces.

We first saw the survivors as they marched down the Lagerstrasse on their way to the Catholic Church on their first Sunday in the camp. Boys of sixteen and men of sixty and over marched with pride and discipline, knowing that through the eyes of their fellow prisoners they represented their country to the world. They received an ovation throughout their march from all nationalities and ranks. It was a very emotional experience.

The German attitude towards them was another paradox. They were treated as privileged prisoners and with great respect.

There were now three groups of Poles in the camp: the Poles captured at the beginning of the war who were treated appallingly; those captured in British uniform who were treated as British, and those captured at Warsaw who were treated as heroes.

Towards the end of November, 1944, we began to realize that our hopes of 'being home by Christmas' were waning. Why is it that in every war soldiers clutch at the hope of 'being home by Christmas'? I suppose it is because Christmas is a time for home and family. Anyway we resigned ourselves to the inevitable and our group began to rehearse our panto-mime. We had decided on Cinderella and I had cast myself as the Fairy Queen. The script was very basic consisting mostly of lavatorial couplets. My breasts were a couple of German lavatory rolls wrapped up in a 'bra' made from an army shirt and my exit line after the Transformation Scene was:

> Once again I've done my bit!
> I think I'll go and have a shit!

Removing one 'breast' from my bra and exiting on tiptoes Stage Left! My entrance line at the end of the show was:

> Our Panto is over –
> The story is told
> My God – those bloody seats are cold!

followed by a high-kicking version of 'Stay in My Arms Cinderella' performed by the entire cast.

On Christmas Eve we had a surprise visitor in our hut. Not Father Christmas but a Russian Officer who, at great personal risk, had climbed over the wires between our compounds to present the British Officers with a mandolin. It had been beautifully made out of wood cut from their hut walls and they had found a piece of brass to engrave their thanks for the Red Cross food we had given them over the months.

On Christmas morning all the Russians stood by the wire and sang carols to us. Their voices were quite outstanding and it was very moving – particularly as we knew they were all under sentence of death from Stalin when the war was over. It was a good start to a day which somehow or other we made very much a Christmas. I had made a Christmas pudding out of German bread, porridge, condensed milk and raisins which I boiled in a sock for hours. It badly needed brandy. We had bought two bottles of quite disgusting wine with cigarettes and an American called 'Casey' Jones had made a 'liqueur' in his home-made still which, as a drink, was a very good emetic! The Germans had even made some 'near' beer available, so we all got quite merry.

January was a very bleak month. Red Cross parcels had run out completely and the weather was terribly cold. The only way to keep warm was to lie on the bunks all day after Appell.

We were now getting very overcrowded as the Germans began marching in prisoners from camps over-run by the Allies. Our bed-blocks now consisted of twelve bunks – three up by two wide and two long. The top bunks were up to the ceiling. There was only a narrow aisle down the centre of the hut. Our theatre had gone, of course, to take more prisoners.

On 26 January as we lay talking on our bunks I suddenly realized that it was my 24th birthday. When I told the others they asked what I would be doing if I were in London.

'I'd treat you all to a bloody good dinner!'

We played the Menu game. We often did it. In turn we all pretended we were ordering a meal in a famous restaurant. As it was my birthday I was allowed to kick off.

'We'll start with a dozen Colchester oysters – lemon only – no bloody Tabasco rubbish – and we'll drink Chablis with them. Then we'll have rump steaks cooked au poivre with lashings of cream and brandy – served with freshly picked baby Scarlet Runner beans and new potatoes smothered in butter and chives. We'll drink La Tâche with that. Then we'll have strawberries and Devonshire cream accompanied by Beaune de Venise and finish up with Stilton, high-baked water biscuits and celery – of course with vintage port!'

There was a long pause as we all savoured the imaginary meal. Then a Canadian Captain called MacDonald in the bunk above me asked: 'How much would you spend per head?

'Oh – at least a fiver!'

'Tell you what – I've saved up a K-ration chocolate bar. It's yours for a fiver!'

'Done!'

I wrote him out a cheque on a piece of German lavatory paper, heading it Barclay's Bank, Piccadilly Circus, where I had my main account. He handed over the chocolate and I ate it very slowly telling the others which course I was eating.

'These are the oysters – a bit more lemon, please, waiter . . .' and so on until the bar was finished. The others appeared to enjoy it with me.

Some weeks after the war my Bank Manager telephoned.

'Mr Bond – a most extraordinary document has been presented through the Royal Bank of Canada . . .'

'Pay it!'

As Hitler's German Empire shrank with the Allies advancing from the west and the Russians from the east, whole prison camps were marched into Moosberg and the situation began to be very alarming. We were living in increasingly cramped conditions and the sanitation was beginning to break down. The overworked Shit Machine just couldn't keep pace with our output and the stench from the latrine permeated the whole compound.

Keeping free of lice was very important because it was rumoured that typhus had broken out in the Russian other ranks' compound. When any British Officer became lousy everyone joined in to help by scrubbing him all over with strong German soap and boiling all his clothes in food ration buckets. The resulting liquid was called Lice Soup!

As the population of the camp grew so did the population of bed bugs. These revolting creatures dwelt in the woodwork of the bed-blocks and emerged at night to gorge themselves on our blood. They loved ankles, so it was essential to tuck ones Long John pants well into one's socks which were always worn in bed. Of course the more intrepid bed bug would always find his way through the Y-front of the pants where there were rich pickings indeed!

We frequently conducted a bed bug blitz by holding a flaming torch of paper under all the joints of the bed-block for as long as we dared without setting fire to the whole thing. The resulting snap, crackle and pop would have made a splendid commercial for Kellogg's Rice Krispies!

We received information that the Nazis were intending to hold out in what was called the Bavarian Redoubt. We were in the middle of it. The intention was apparently to assemble as many Officer prisoners as possible in the Redoubt and for senior Nazis to use them as hostages for their safe conduct. This was a very worrying thought and we decided that if the situation ever deteriorated to the point where hostages were shot we would try and take over the camp. It was a wild notion but we were determined to make a stand should the worst come to the worst.

As if to reinforce our fears for the future, we were told that the SS had taken over command of the camp and that a high-ranking SS General was about to make a tour of inspection. He arrived late one afternoon while we were all lying on our bunks trying to keep warm. An Oberfeldwebel who had apparently heard the shout 'Goon up!' and thought it was an English call to Attention threw open our hut doors.

'*Goon up!*' he shouted.

The General strutted in to be greeted by hysterical laughter from the hundreds of British Officers crammed into the hut. He didn't like it at all.

Our original 175 Officers had stuck together although we were totally outnumbered by prisoners from other camps – many of whom had been prisoners for up to five years. Their attitude towards the Germans was much more tolerant than ours. A great deal about them was different. Many of them had arrived in the camp with prams, wheelbarrows and other 'vehicles' crammed with possessions they had acquired over the years. It didn't seem to occur to them that we were likely to be liberated soon and all their 'things' would be just so much junk. Even their Kriegie language was different. For instance they called stoofahs spiffers! Terribly ignorant!

I had one terrible worry nagging away at me ever since I was taken prisoner. My wife had been three months' pregnant when I flew out to rejoin the Battalion. How had she taken the shock of the telegram? I had particular reason to worry. Just before D-Day my brother Kenneth had been commanding a Squadron of Halifaxes from Elvington in Yorkshire. On his very last mission before a rest period he was shot down over France. My sister-in-law, Margaret, was three months' pregnant and when she received the telegram – '. . . regret to inform you . . . missing in action', everyone in the family hastened to reassure her. He was either a POW or would suddenly turn up having been helped to escape by the French Resistance.

I was still at Mons Barracks at this time and one morning I got an urgent call to meet my father in London. A Flight Sergeant who had been my brother's rear gunner had made it back to England. Father and I met him over lunch. He did not have good news. Apparently, after dropping their bombs on the marshalling yards at Laon, they were attacked by German fighters and badly hit. Kenneth himself was wounded. His last words to the crew were: 'All right, chaps – abandon aircraft! Abandon aircraft! Good luck!'

The sergeant told me that the whole crew except my brother

were able to jump but that there was no way Kenneth could have got out.

After the sergeant had left us, my father and I agreed that Margaret should not be told but allowed to complete her pregnancy with a little hope to hang on to. My wife Ann was privy to this family conspiracy. Now she too was pregnant and she would have received the telegram – '. . . husband, Captain D. W. D. Bond, is missing in action.'!

I had received no letters since I had been taken prisoner but had written my full quota to Ann. Suddenly in late March I received a whole batch of letters together. They were all from my wife. The latest one was dated 20 January. I opened it frantically and read: 'I have just put Anthony to bed after his six-o'clock bath.'

I had a son.

As the conditions within the camp deteriorated, with hundreds of additional prisoners arriving almost daily, it was only the rumours of the rapidly approaching American Army that kept our spirits up.

It was cold, becoming increasingly smelly and the over-crowding was so acute that it was like living every twenty-four hours of the day in a football crowd. It was impossible to be alone – ever – not even in the latrine. We drank a lot of fluid to fill our stomachs so we were trekking out to the latrine to pee all night. The latrine always seemed to be full and there were always a stream of Kriegies on the way out and on the way back. The clatter of this constant traffic was made worse by wooden clogs which many of us wore because, for some strange reason, they were warmer than our boots which, in any case, were by now very worn.

Even walking round the compound became a bit of a nightmare. Our compound had always turned right out of the hut and walked round anti-clockwise. It was considered very anti-social to walk round clockwise because groups walking in opposite directions were constantly having to make way for each other. Apparently in some other camps it was customary to walk clockwise and so the newcomers became an irritant to us. The polite 'Sorry!' and 'Excuse me!' rapidly deteriorated into '*Do* fuck off!'

Relations between the different nationalities began to get rather ragged, too, with the strain we were all under. For instance when the Senior British Officer was told by an American Southerner Colonel that he didn't want the Red Cross to be run by a 'goddamned Nigger!', it was frigidly pointed out to him that Kiwi was a British Officer and that his colour was immaterial.

Americans from other parts of the United States were just as shocked by the Southerner's behaviour as we were. However, it was noticeable that Canadian Kriegies who had been markedly 'North American' when the camp was mainly British became very Commonwealth as more Americans poured into the camp. The South Africans had always been very pro-British and I made some good friends among them.

As whole camps from other parts of Germany arrived in Moosberg we became a rather insignificant little group. Our SBO, for instance, was well down the pecking order and no longer in command. The other camps had all been so well-established and organized that they took charge. Our 175 were swamped by them and we became 'the forgotten men'. We were the last to get any information at a time when Moosberg was alive with rumours.

It was said, for instance, that the new Senior British Officer was in negotiation with the Commandant and the local SS Commander to take over the camp. From this further rumours flooded. The Germans *were* handing over the camp to us . . . The Germans were *not* going to hand over to us . . . The Wehrmacht *wanted* to hand over to us . . . The SS *refused* to let the Wehrmacht hand over to us. Our compound only got reports at fifth or sixth hand and they were always very garbled and unconvincing.

On 24 April Oflag VIIb arrived from Eichstatt after a horrendous march. This was the Officers' camp we had originally been destined for but never reached. Perhaps it was just as well. Their column had formed up outside their camp ready to march off when some American Thunderbolt fighters came over and, mistaking the prisoners for an enemy column, machine-gunned them relentlessly. Eight British prisoners were killed and forty-two wounded.

Among the Eichstatt prisoners was an actor called Wally Douglas who had run the theatre in VIIb for over four years. Somebody introduced me to him as the impressario of Moosburg! He had become so conditioned to being a POW that he clearly found it difficult to accept the fact that liberation was near. Believe it or not, at this late stage he wanted us to get down to work at once putting on shows. Even when I showed him what used to be our theatre now crammed with Kriegies from wall to wall and floor to ceiling he wanted to explore the possibilities of outdoor theatre. After the war Wally directed some of London's most successful farces at the Whitehall Theatre.

Our secret wireless was being openly operated by now but the BBC bulletins were well behind actual events in the battlefield so we were very much in the dark as to when we could expect to be liberated. Political news, like the report of Mussolini's execution on 28 April, gave us great cheer and it was clear that Berlin had virtually fallen. However, we were in the Bavarian Redoubt with all those Nazis around us. Our Kriegie caution made us wary of overoptimism.

VII

Liberation

At dawn on 29 April, among further rumours that the British had now taken over the camp, I staggered out to the latrine with a score of other Kriegies for my first pee of the day. Certainly the Germans were still in the tiger boxes on our part of the perimeter wire. As we stood there in rows obtaining our relief we heard an outburst of automatic firing.

'Christ! What's that?'

A pessimist said, 'Firing range up at the airfield!'

There was another burst of firing.

'That's not a German weapon – too slow a rate of fire!'

We all dashed out into the compound. Prisoners were hurrying out of all the hundreds of huts throughout the camp. The camp had been built by French POWs in 1940 for 10,000 prisoners. We were now at least 100,000. Many of the fences dividing the compounds had been pulled down and all the Kriegies massed together on the higher ground to get the best view. It was quite a sight.

Beyond the wire to the west of the camp there was open ground and cultivated land including our personally fertilized cabbage field. Beyond that the ground rose towards a pine forest on the skyline the other side of a shallow valley. The firing was coming from that direction. There was another burst of firing and the sunlight glistened on something metallic emerging from the trees. An American standing next to me shouted: 'It's a Sherman! It's a goddam Sherman tank!'

It was!

Things really hotted up after that. An SS Division was

fighting in the area and they put up a fanatical resistance. The battle raged all round the camp and several times when bullets cracked across the compounds prisoners dived for cover. It looked like a field of corn being mown down. At one point there was a series of explosions which seemed to us to come from within the camp towards the main guardroom. They had. We discovered later that a group of young Nazis from the SS had rushed into the camp and ordered our guards to come out and fight. The Volkssturm weren't having any of it.

'*Krieg verloren!*'

Whereupon the Nazis threw hand grenades into the guardroom, killing several of the old boys and wounding others.

Suddenly the firing stopped. There was a long period of silence. We all emerged from our huts. Looking towards the cheese factory in the town of Moosberg we saw the Stars and Stripes being hauled up on the flagpole. My American friend had tears streaming down his face.

'My aching balls! The Flag!'

We were free.

The sentries climbed down from their tiger boxes and marched rapidly towards the main gate, one or two of them throwing their helmets over the wire as souvenirs for the prisoners.

The Sonderführer came scuttling into our compound and tried to surrender to the SBO, because he was afraid, so he said, of his fellow SS officers. He was sent packing.

By this time the cheering was deafening and prisoners emerged from all over the camp bearing their national flags which had been made in secret. Men climbed on to the roofs waving them and shouting – British, American, French, Polish, Greek, Russian flags.

After a bit an American jeep and a Sherman tank moved slowly down the Lagerstrasse. You could hardly see the tank for prisoners climbing all over it. Nearly all the 100,000 prisoners were crying, but not so much as the tank crew who had tears pouring down their cheeks. We did not realize how thin and strained we all looked and our appearance must have been a shock to our liberators.

The days that followed were a terrible anticlimax after the euphoria of liberation. We were asked to remain in the camp until proper arrangements could be made for our repatriation. The Russian prisoners broke out of the camp and caused mayhem and murder throughout the farming community around Moosberg – raping the women, plundering the houses and slaughtering the cattle. A huge Cossack private came into our compound wearing a woman's fur coat and hat and dragging the carcass of a pig behind him. He sawed off a leg with a German bayonet and offered it to us.

Things got so bad that American troops had to round up the Russians and drive them back into the camp by force of arms. Unobtrusively an American Officer allowed us to make a small gap in our wire on condition that we used it with discretion and did not all flood out at once. He also warned us of the danger of trying to make our own way back to the West. There were pockets of hard-line Nazis called the Werewolves who would shoot us on sight if we stumbled across them. It was clearly more sensible to wait for an orderly evacuation of the camp.

We agreed to take it in turn by syndicates to have an hour in the woods. When it was our syndicate's turn the five of us walked out and without a word between us went our separate ways. I walked off into the pine forest and found a clearing in the sunlight. I sat on a fallen tree and smoked a cigarette. It was the first time I had been alone for eight months. It was the most peaceful hour of my life.

General Patton, whose troops, to our intense relief, had moved too rapidly for the Nazis to set up their Bavarian Redoubt, visited the camp and walked the whole length of the Lagerstrasse with two pearl-handled pistols riding up and down aggressively on his buttocks. He received an ovation which he obviously relished.

Because Patton's lines of communication were so stretched the American's were not able to do very much about our rations at first. All they could do was to round up as many Red Cross parcels as possible and distribute them, but with the numbers in the camp so swollen they didn't go very far.

To our astonishment one day a Mobile Doughnut Factory appeared in the Lagerstrasse accompanied by a Senator who, it appears, had made his millions out of doughnuts. It was manned by some very nubile young women in uniform. The factory went into production and thousands of prisoners crowded round. After distributing a maximum of 1,000 doughnuts among 100,000 prisoners they had presumably obtained all the publicity photographs and film that the Senator required for what was clearly a promotional exercise. The Doughnut Factory then withdrew to a storm of barracking from the disenchanted Kriegies.

Six days after our liberation a more serious-minded Senator visited the camp and was shocked at the conditions we were still living under. Apparently he had some very strong and effective words to say to the Allied Command and at long last things began to move.

A huge convoy of big open trucks driven by broadly smiling negroes began to ferry us to the airfield at Landshut. The journey was terrifying as the drivers had obviously been told to step on the gas to speed up the turnround.

At the airfield we formed a massive queue right round the perimeter. Dakotas were landing and taking off at an amazing rate.

One tragedy occurred when a landing plane blew a tyre and crashed into a loaded plane taking off. It was a terrible sight to see men who had been liberated after months and even years of captivity leaping out of the plane with their clothes on fire.

Another hazard was the presence near the airfield of Were-wolves. A group of them started firing at our massive queue. American infantry units were rushed in and we were filled with admiration at their skill, bravery and sheer ruthlessness in tackling the Nazis.

Although we had reached Landshut at first light it was clear by the evening that we weren't going to make it that night. When trucks were brought up to drive us back to our camp in Moosberg we refused. We said we would prefer to sleep in the open. When it was clear to the Americans that we had no intention of returning to Moosberg, they reluctantly accepted it and we started to settle down under any cover we could find.

A high-ranking American General was driving past and stopped when he saw us.

'Who the hell are these?'

'POWs awaiting repatriation, Sir.'

'What the hell are they doing sleeping in the open?'

He took immediate charge and gave orders that blocks of flats in the nearby town of Landshut were to be evacuated by all German civilians except the old and sick. The Germans were to put fresh linen on all their beds and get out within half an hour. We were to be moved in.

Our little group didn't much like the look of the block of workers' flats where most of the POWs were being billeted and found a rather smarter flat which, with the help of a young American Lieutenant, we appropriated. He also provided us with some splendid rations. We allowed an old German to remain. He was terrified of us at first but when we asked him to share our meal with us he relaxed a bit. He even produced some schnapps and a few bottles of wine.

It was an extraordinary experience lying in a bed with clean sheets again and I didn't sleep at all.

The following day towards afternoon we reached the head of the queue and boarded a Dakota which flew us to Lille in northern France. The Americans had organized everything splendidly. We were driven to an enormous tented town and led straight to the Mess marquee. We had always thought that we would be fed on rice and other bland foods at first because our stomachs had shrunk. Apparently it was considered that the psychological considerations were more important. We were fed asparagus, roast chicken, roast potatoes, peas and beans, followed by fresh fruit and ice-cream.

To round it off we had real coffee, cheese and biscuits and a large cigar! That night I did sleep!

The following day we were handed over to the British for transport back to England. The cynical among us anticipated a return to a British Army 'cock-up'! How wrong we were. We were crowded on to Lancaster bombers and I managed to get a place by the bomb aimer's window. The planes deliberately flew us over the white cliffs of Dover and then made a low circuit of London before landing at an airfield in Buckinghamshire.

As we disembarked from the plane there were three Senior Officers of each Service to shake us by the hand.

'Welcome home!'

We were then led to a huge hangar bedecked with Union Jacks and bunting. Inside we had to submit to yet another 'de-lousing' which consisted of a squirt of de-lousing powder under the armpits and around the crutch. It had been done by the Americans at Moosberg and again at Landshut – but they weren't taking any chances.

As we moved into the main part of the hangar it was difficult to control our emotions. There were rows of trestle tables beautifully laid for tea with flowers everywhere. To serve us were WVS, WRNS, ATS and WAAFs. They were the first British women we had seen for months and they all looked beautiful. As they fussed over us in a motherly way I could hardly bring myself to speak because I was afraid I would cry.

After a magnificent English tea of paste and cucumber sandwiches, home-made cakes and real tea with real milk and real sugar we were invited to wait for our transport to transit centres. Even the waiting had been thought out with great sensitivity. For months on end none of us had even seen an easy chair. We had been sitting on benches or on the edges of our bunks in bed-blocks of twelve. Rows and rows of easy chairs had been arranged with a small table beside each chair loaded with all the recent magazines and copies of the day's newspapers. It was VE Day!

With as little delay as possible we were organized into truckloads to be driven to our transit areas. Once again the organizers had excelled themselves and along all the routes the public in every village, town and hamlet had been asked to turn out and give the POWs a welcome home. More tears.

The transit area I was sent to was a large country house which had been turned into a centre for an Officers' course. The Officers attending the course had been sent home on leave and we moved in. I was particularly touched when a Guards Mess Sergeant gently relieved me of my pathetic little bundle of possessions.

'May I, Sir? I'll show you to your room.'

He then issued me with a suit of denims and with carefully controlled distaste removed my filthy POW battledress to be destroyed. He ran me a hot bath and I felt clean for the first time since I was captured.

After a painless de-briefing by Intelligence Officers we were told the Officers' Mess bar was open and that later that evening there would be an ENSA concert down in the Mess Hall. I had a large whisky and took my place in the queue for the telephone. I got through to my wife.

'Darling – I'm home and I'm safe!'

After a very emotional telephone conversation with my son gurgling away in the background my wife suddenly said: 'By the way – Ealing Studios have been telephoning every day to see if you were home. They have a film for you straight away!'

It was *The Captive Heart*, set in a prison camp and eight weeks later I was back in Germany on location in an identical prison camp to Moosberg playing the part of a POW!

I needed another whisky to recover from this shock and while I was sipping it with relish in the bar I picked up a copy of *The Illustrated London News*. To my astonishment there was a long article about Ealing Studios.

'Ealing Studios are shortly to embark on one of their most ambitious films to date – *Nicholas Nickleby* by Charles Dickens. Sir Cedric Hardwicke has been contracted to play Ralph Nickleby and other star artists are to be Stanley

Holloway, Bernard Miles, Fay Compton and Sally Ann Howes is to play Kate. A young unknown actor called Derek Bond has been cast as Nicholas but he is a prisoner of war and it is not yet known if he is safe.'

I had to read it three times before I could believe it. What a welcome home!

WVS ladies were busily sewing our badges of rank, designations and medal ribbons on brand new battledresses. While this was happening I thought I would look at the ENSA concert. In the little camp theatre there were only about 30 men in the audience and just before the curtain went up I noticed one of the cast peeping through to 'count the house' – no doubt out of force of habit after years of playing at the end of the pier.

There was a very loud intro on a tinny upright piano and the curtains parted to reveal a middle-aged Pierrot group which stridently burst into song.

'You've . . . got . . . to . . . SMILE!!'

I knew I was home.

When I had collected my new uniform and been issued with a Ration Card and £10 cash I was just about to return to the bar when a WVS lady came up to me.

'Excuse me, but aren't you Derek Bond?'

I was astonished to be recognized.

'Well . . . yes.'

'We met years ago – I play bridge with your mother. I live in Farnham Royal. I've nearly finished here – would you like me to drive you home? I'm sure they'll allow it.'

They did. I just couldn't believe my luck. I telephoned my mother so that my arrival would not be too much of a shock and we set off. When I walked up to the front door of our house called Camelot I heard the sounds of a party. Typically my father had hurriedly arranged a Welcome Home party with all the neighbours including John Clements, Kay Hammond and Diana Morgan from Ealing Studios. It was all too much for me. As I walked into the room I burst into tears.

The following morning I went to Paddington Station to meet my wife and son, Anthony, off the train from Bristol. I felt very nervous and on edge. It was a strange reunion. Ann looked at me with undisguised shock on her face but quickly recovered and hugged me. When she had received the telegram she had, as I had feared, assumed I was dead and had adjusted herself to that. This man hugging her on Paddington Station must have seemed like a very skinny stranger. My son Anthony gave me a big toothless grin and belched loudly when I kissed him.

I wasted no time in going along to Ealing Studios the day after Ann's arrival. I got a tremendously warm welcome from the Studio. Michael Balcon told me that they had already applied for my release to do the film and confirmed that I was to play *Nicholas Nickleby* afterwards. There was no problem with the Army. I was given indefinite leave until my demobilization and I was attached to Wellington Barracks for pay and rations. I was allowed to use the Officers' Mess as often as I wished.

My relations with my wife I knew would take time and I soon discovered that the physical aspect of our life was decidedly one-sided. However, she had Anthony to absorb her interests and affection and I had my career.

Margaret Bonnar, the Casting Director at Ealing, and Diana Morgan realized I needed a lot of help to adjust to civilian life after prison camp and were immensely supportive. They had taken on quite a task. Many ex-POWs required psychiatric treatment and I counted myself lucky to have the support of good friends and a loving family.

It is difficult to explain but I felt very gauche and insecure. I couldn't seem to enter into intelligent conversation at first and sat among people feeling like a bore.

I found myself spending more and more time in the Mess at Wellington Barracks where I felt relaxed and at home. I'm sure that many Service men and women felt the same as I did for some time after the war and that is why so many little drinking clubs opened up.

They were phoney little 'Officers' Messes' where the mal-adjusted could console each other. They were particularly used by ex-Service people whose social background had been fundamentally changed by their wartime careers.

While I was looking for a home before I started filming I stayed with my parents in Farnham Royal. As I was shortly going off on location it seemed sensible for Ann to return to Bristol with Anthony and rejoin me when I had found a home of our own.

Diana Morgan did everything she could to establish me in the film world, including arranging a party for Michael Balcon, John Clements, Kay Hammond and others to which I was asked. Many of the people there were well established stars that I hadn't heard of and I dropped a large brick with a good-looking man who sat next to me at a table horse-racing game. He looked at me with total disinterest and said:

'Who are you?'

'My name's Bond. Who are you?'

It brought the house down. He was Stewart Granger.

It seemed no time at all before the Ealing Studio *Captive Heart* unit set off for location in Germany. I was deeply apprehensive.

As I boarded the Dakota at Landshut in Bavaria on VE Day minus one, I had sworn, in common with most other POWs, that I would never set foot in Germany again. Here I was only a few weeks later boarding another Dakota to fly back to Germany. I have to admit that my heart was thumping very hard when we landed at an airfield outside Hamburg.

The camp we were going to use was at a place called Westertimke halfway between Hamburg and Bremen. It was the camp from which the famous 'Albert RN' escape had taken place when British Naval POWs had built a 'dummy' Kriegie to take on Appell and cover for an escaped POW.

We were to stay at a small hotel in the centre of the market town which was rather like an English pub. It was a decidedly eerie feeling walking through the main gates of the camp on the first day of shooting. All the débris left by the departing POWs was littered about – stoofahs, home-made frying pans and other artefacts made from Red Cross parcel tins.

My fellow actors, Michael Redgrave, Basil Radford and Gordon Jackson among them, were very kind and understanding towards me, but I still felt uneasy.

One day when I had a bit of time off during shooting I walked into an empty compound next to the one being used for the film. I walked round and round – anti-clockwise of course. I continued to walk round the compound until I induced in myself the belief that the liberation – the journey home – Ealing Studios – my family welcome had all been a dream and that I really was still a prisoner. Then I turned and walked straight out of the main gates of the camp. I let out a great sigh of relief. I sat and smoked a cigarette and then strolled happily back behind the barbed wire. From then on I was able to face up to the location.

The extras in the film were soldiers from the Argyll and Sutherland Highlanders and the Black Watch, from the 51st Highland Division. They were a very tough bunch indeed and rather 'bolshie', as they all wanted to be sent home. Some of them, after all, had fought their way all the way from Alamein and up through Italy before being switched to France and Germany. Their mood wasn't helped by Basil Dearden, the director, trying to do a 'Monty' and wearing both regimental badges in his beret. This and the monotony of repeating shots over and over again almost brought them to the point of mutiny.

One night the Sergeants' Mess of the Argyll and Sutherlands invited all the actors for drinks. The purpose was to get us all legless drunk and they succeeded. The evening ended with a very tough Sergeant-Major singing 'Jerusalem' with more enthusiasm than talent. This was too much for the sentimental Basil Radford who, with tears of almost neat schnapps pouring down his cheeks, said: 'They've fought all the way from Alamein and now – now they're singing Jerusalem!'

The last I remember of the evening was Basil being supported back to our hotel by two Highland sergeants singing 'There'll Always Be an England!'

On a day off Basil and I went into Hamburg. The Atlantic Hotel had miraculously survived the devastating bombing and was used as an Officers' Club. We were drinking in the bar with some other officers when we heard on the radio the news that an atomic bomb had been dropped on Hiroshima. We were stunned by the news and, although we had all been fighting soldiers – Basil had flown fighters in the Royal Flying Corps during World War I – we were all rather shocked. When you realize that the news meant that almost certainly the war against Japan would soon be over and therefore those of us still serving would not be sent to the Far East it was quite a remarkable reaction.

By the time we had returned to England to complete the film in the studios Japan had surrendered. The War was over.

With the backing of Ealing Studios I applied to the Regiment for their assistance in getting me released from the Army. It was granted. I was a civilian again.

Epilogue

German soldiers commonly said to their captives with some envy: 'For you the war is over!'

Even forty-five years after VE Day the war is not over for many ex-Service people – some because they hark back to the war years as the most exciting and fulfilling time of their lives – others because the war has left scars either physical or mental which will never heal.

When I was wounded on 19 December, 1942, Guardsman Woodward had to take his place as an ordinary Rifleman in No 4 Platoon because my replacement brought his own servant with him. He managed to survive the Tunisian campaign but once the Battalion became heavily engaged in battle in Italy his nerve finally failed him. His mental funkhole was to convince himself that all the horrors of battle were merely a major exercise with live ammunition and that soon the Battalion would be returning to billets in Perth where we had been stationed before sailing for North Africa. His fellow Guardsmen weren't psychiatrists and thought it all rather a joke: 'Listen! Old Woodward's on about Perth again!'

It was no joke and Woodward was sent back to England seriously mentally ill. He appeared to recover and resumed his pre-war job in a paper mill near Aylesbury. One night he went berserk and savagely attacked his wife with a broken milk bottle. An Officer from Regimental Headquarters appeared for him at his trial to give evidence of his problems. He was given a suspended sentence and bound over on condition that he voluntarily underwent treatment in a mental hospital.

I had attempted to visit him but had been told by his doctors that the wartime associations might be too disturbing for him.

One night early in 1946 I was studying for tomorrow's heavy day's filming on *Nicholas Nickleby* at my new home in East Twickenham. Suddenly there was a thunderous hammering at the front door. It was pouring with rain. I opened the door to find Woodward standing there without an overcoat and soaking wet. He was also extremely agitated. I calmed him down and while my wife made some hot tea I gave him some dry clothes and sat him in front of the fire. Once my wife had brought him the tea he stopped shivering and began talking rapidly. It was a stream of reminiscence of our training in Scotland. He had taken a liking to Ann and began an embarrassing eulogy to her about 'his Officer'.

When it seemed safe to leave him for a moment I went up to my room and looked up my Grenadier Guards Comrade's Association book. I had been writing to Woodward at a Mental Hospital in Aylesbury. I looked up the Aylesbury Branch. The Secretary was an Inspector of Police. I telephoned the Police Station. The Inspector was off duty and naturally the Station Officer refused to give me his home number but agreed to telephone him and give him a message.

'Tell him that Captain Bond, Grenadier Guards, telephoned and that I've got Guardsman Woodward in my home in a very agitated state!'

The Inspector rang back in no time at all.

'Keep him calm, Sir, whatever you do. He can still be violent. I'll tell you what I've done . . .'

He had contacted the Kingston Police unofficially and discovered that two CID men were also ex-Grenadiers. They were on their way.

When they arrived we had a hasty whispered conversation on the front doorstep.

'Does he know you telephoned, Sir?'

'Don't think so!'

'Good. We were just passing on duty, Sir, and thought we'd look up an old Grenadier! Right, Sir?'

They handled it beautifully, Woodward didn't seem to suspect a thing and the evening developed into a Grenadier reunion. In due course one of the CID men said: 'We're off now, Sir. Woodward – we're going up Aylesbury way. Would you like a lift?'

Woodward went like a lamb and was smuggled back into his mental home with nothing on the record.

Sadly, after he had appeared to recover and been discharged from hospital he became an alcoholic. Major 'Fwed' Turner, the Regimental Welfare Officer, did everything he could to help but to no avail. Eventually the Salvation Army took over his case but he died a 'wino'.

After our capture on Florence Racecourse in August, 1944, I had often wondered about Aldo, the Partisan. He had excused himself from the luncheon and was absent for about twenty minutes. Had he 'set up' our capture? There were times when I was convinced that he had, but Joshua Rowley always vigorously defended him.

In April, 1989, Joshua Rowley, John Pearson-Gregory and I lunched together at the Garrick Club. It was the first time I had seen John since our capture. The last I had seen of him on that day was his back view as he leapt over a wall and raced to freedom. He made his way back to the Battalion and was badly wounded at Monte Battaglia.

Over our coffee I brought up the subject of Aldo and John gave me his account of what had happened to him. Apparently Aldo had managed to escape from the Germans very early on and made his way to the *casa* of some family friends. They gave him fresh clothes and when it seemed safe they got him back to his family in 11 Via Magenta, Florence. However, the Germans tracked him down and recaptured him. He was put on trial as a traitor and condemned to death. The Germans even erected a scaffold in Prato for a public execution to discourage other Italian Officers from defecting to the allies.

A high-ranking Roman Catholic priest intervened and begged the Germans for Aldo's life. The Germans relented and changed Aldo's sentence to life imprisonment. Aldo escaped once again and returned to Florence where by this time his home was firmly in Allied hands.

If this account is true, and I have no reason to doubt it, the question arises – Why didn't the Provost Marshal warn us that the Via Magenta was not in Allied hands when he issued us with a pass for the Bailey bridge? We told him our destination. Why were there no road blocks at the limits of the British positions? These omissions cost Joshua and me our freedom for eight long months.

For Lew Kurolowitz, the Polish Officer who joined our syndicate when Jock had departed, hugging his sixth of a parcel to his chest, the war didn't end on his return to Britain. His wife had been a hospital consultant on tuberculosis on the outbreak of war and had joined a Military Hospital. She was captured by the Germans when Poland collapsed and made to work for a German Military Hospital. The last that Lew had heard of her was that she had been captured by the Russians at Stalingrad. With the help of the International Red Cross she was finally tracked down in a Refugee Camp and brought back to England to be reunited with Lew.

Unfortunately she had absolutely no documentary proof of her high medical qualifications. The ex-Kriegie 'old boy' network went into action and, largely through Joshua Rowley's efforts, she sat some exams and was allowed to practise. Lew in the meantime became a glider Instructor teaching RAF flying cadets and other young people.

I lost touch with them completely so I was very shocked in 1985 to receive news from one of Lew's cadets that he had died very tragically. Apparently his wife had died suddenly from a heart attack. Lew was inconsolable. He had lost his country and now he had lost his wife. He piled her grave with flowers and then lay down among them and shot himself with a Service revolver.

On 8 July, 1960, I attended a very sad occasion at Buckingham Palace. Her Majesty The Queen as Colonel-in-Chief of the Grenadiers was taking the Farewell Parade of the Third Battalion which was being disbanded.

The Battalion Colour was to be handed over to the Inkerman Company attached to the Second Battalion so that its history could be kept in continuity in the event of the Third Battalion ever being reformed. There are forty-four Battle Honours on the Colour starting with Tangier in 1680 right through Waterloo, Inkerman, the Somme, Dunkirk, Medjez and the Gothic Line.

It was a very emotional moment as I stood next to my former Company Commander, Kenny Tufnell, to watch the Battalion slow march off the Parade Ground into history.

The five of us in the Syndicate all had full civilian lives to resume. Joshua Rowley inherited his father's baronetcy and became the Lord-Lieutenant of Suffolk. Jasper Grinling became Managing Director of a large distillery group and remained as a Director when it was taken over by Metropolitan Hotels. Peter Langdon-Davies resumed a successful career at the Bar. Rupert Woolcombe became a country solicitor. My film career really took off after the success of *Nicholas Nickleby*.

In 1975 Peter Langdon-Davies suggested that we have a reunion. I contacted the *Evening Standard* to cover the story with the others' consent. The newspaper had a blow-up of a photograph taken of us in Moosberg by a guard shortly before we were liberated and the now rather portly syndicate posed underneath it in the same physical attitudes that we had assumed in Germany. The *Evening Standard* devoted half a page to the story.

It was 29 April, 1975 – exactly thirty years after we had been liberated. We set off to a splendid French Restaurant and ordered the meal we had all dreamed about in Moosberg. We all failed miserably to eat our way through it!

One of the great advantages of being an actor is that you work on equal terms with people of all ages. There is no doubt that it helps to keep actors young in heart.

I have been struck over recent years by the renewed interest shown in the Second World War by young people in their twenties. After fifty years it is, of course, now history to them. Many young actors and actresses I have worked with ply me with questions about the War. They are not interested in Generals or the movements of divisions and armies. Nor do they care all that much about the political background to the War.

They seem to want to know what it was like to be young and at war.

That is why I have written this book. I hope I have been able to give some flavour of the period as well as recall some of my wartime experiences and show something of the influence five years of war had on an impressionable young man of nineteen.